Chartered Banker

PRACTICE & REVISION KIT
Contemporary Issues in Banking

In this 2014/15 edition

- A **user-friendly format** for easy navigation
- **Updated** on recent developments
- **Question practice on each chapter** to test knowledge retention
- **Exam-standard** mock examinations

Chartered Banker
Leading financial professionalism

BPP
LEARNING MEDIA

Published July 2014

ISBN 978 1 4727 0505 1

British Library Cataloguing-in-Publication Data
A catalogue record for this book
is available from the British Library

Published by

BPP Learning Media Ltd
BPP House, Aldine Place
London W12 8AA

www.bpp.com/learningmedia

Printed in United Kingdom by Ricoh UK Limited

Unit 2,
Wells Place,
Merstham,
RH1 3LG

Your learning materials, published by BPP Learning Media
Ltd, are printed on paper obtained from traceable
sustainable sources.

CONTENTS

	Page	
	Questions	**Answers**

Q u e s t i o n   B a n k

Chapter 1 – Financial Assets, Liabilities and Intermediaries	3	65
Chapter 2 – National Income	7	67
Chapter 3 – Economic Trends and Management Policies	11	69
Chapter 4 – Monetary Policy and Interest Rate Theories	15	71
Chapter 5 – Inflation and the Housing Market	19	73
Chapter 6 – The International Money Markets and Banks	23	75
Chapter 7 – International Loan and Bond Markets	27	77
Chapter 8 – International Banking Risk	31	79
Chapter 9 – Securitisation and Globalisation	35	81
Chapter 10 – Economic Monetary Union (EMU)	39	83
Chapter 11 – Public Finance	43	85
Chapter 12 – Financial Crisis 2007 - 2009	47	87
Chapter 13 – Bank Regulation	51	89
Chapter 14 – Banking/Financial Environment	55	91
Chapter 15 – Innovation and Technology in Banking	59	93

P r a c t i c e   E x a m i n a t i o n s

Practice Examination 1	95	99
Practice Examination 2	105	109
Practice Examination 3	117	121

QUESTION BANK

Chapter 1 – Financial Assets, Liabilities and Intermediaries

1   **Why is it that a study of a nation's economy and financial system is essential to the study of the much smaller subject of banking?**

A   Because it is always useful to have a good background knowledge

B   Because the banking system is invariably an integral part of the much wider whole that is the national economy

C   Because the economy could not function without the banks

D   Because they are in effect the same thing

2   **In a closed situation, on the balance sheet of a nation, why is it that financial assets on the liabilities side always balance exactly with the financial assets on the other?**

A   They don't, it is just chance

B   Because the money issued by a country must be held by someone in that country

C   Because the cash issued by a country must be held by someone else in that country

D   Because the sheet shows all the assets and all the liabilities held in the country

3   **Why is the public sector in an economy almost invariably in deficit?**

A   Because governments use political rather than financial criteria to govern

B   Because governments tend to spend more than they obtain in taxes

C   Because governments have a better ability to raise credit than individuals

D   Because governments are there for the short term

4   **Financial institutions enable financial systems to operate in balance. Why is this?**

A   Because they act as intermediaries thus putting those with excess funds in touch with those with too little funds

B   Because they have expertise that enables this to happen

C   Because they have access to systems that enable this to happen

D   All of the above

5   **Most financial intermediaries are involved in a process called 'asset transformation' Which of the following best describes this term?**

A   The selling and buying of financial assets

B   The selling and buying of any assets

C   Taking financial assets from one group of owners and making it available to another

D   Borrowing and lending money

6   **In what sense can a financial asset also be a liability?**

A   When it is not paid for by the owner

B   When it is a partly paid share

C   When the owner is a financial intermediary and the liability has been lent on

D   When the owner is a financial intermediary and the asset has been lent on

7   Why do people ask financial intermediaries to accept their assets as liabilities?

A   Because they have confidence in the chosen intermediary

B   Because they feel that this reduces risk to them as owners of the asset

C   Because they obtain a return on the asset that otherwise they would not

D   All of the above

8   Why are the operations of financial intermediaries of great use to large scale borrowers?

A   Because they like to deal with large scale organisations such as banks

B   Because intermediaries are able to aggregate the deposits of many customers to supply the needs of large scale borrowers

C   Because banks have a high level of experience and skill

D   Because banks have an wide range of lending experience and this helps them to make quick lending decisions when a large sum is involved

9   If there were no financial intermediaries, what would happen if those who would be their borrowing customers could not therefore borrow?

A   They could only spend until their money was exhausted

B   They could only spend until they ran out of money

C   They would have to sell all their assets

D   They would have to run down their cash and sell other assets

10   Borrowing long term for short term purchases is precisely what the text books say that customers should not do when using the services of a bank. Yet banks borrow from customers short term and lend long. Why are they able to do this with much less risk of default than are customers?

A   Because of the scale of their operations

B   Because banks are irresponsible and will lend to anyone for anything as long as they make a profit

C   Because of government subsidies

D   Because the Financial Conduct Authority permits this

11   Why are bank balances treated as part of a nation's money supply?

A   Because they are owned by people who live in the country concerned

B   Because the government can seize them in time of need

C   Because they can be used to settle debts in the same way as cash

D   Because they are as liquid as cash

12   Besides the deposit of cash by customers, banks increase the money supply in two other ways. What are these?

A   By lending to the government

B   By the provision of lending facilities to customers

C   Through the money transfer system

D   By the provision of cheques and debit cards to customers

13   How does an absence or shortage of creditworthy borrowers impact on money supply?

A   If the banks cannot lend, then no money will be created by means of credit

B   There will be fewer people to spend

C   There will be fewer people to buy

D   All of the above

14   Which of the following assets of a bank does NOT form part of the liquidity ratio?

A   Loans to triple A rated customers

B   Balances at the Bank of England

C   Gilts

D   Cash

15   Why is the multiplier the reciprocal of the liquidity ratio?

A   Because the multiplier relies ultimately on the availability of liquid cash to work

B   Because they are the same thing

C   Because the multiplier creates the cash that makes up the liquidity ratio

D   All of the above

Chapter 2 – National Income

1   **Around what is national consumption organised?**

A   The use of raw materials by firms

B   The amount that individuals consume

C   The use of utilities by households

D   The amount consumed by households

2   **Around what is the measurement of national production measured?**

A   The amount of raw materials consumed by firms

B   The amount of economic production by firms

C   The amount of production of goods by firms

D   The amount of production by firms that is used by individuals

3   **From what is national income derived?**

A   What everyone in a country earns

B   What all firms in a country earn

C   Income from work done and income from the ownership of land and capital

D   All of the above

4   **Which of the following statements is correct?**

In any national economy, the national income equals

A   Total value of the national production plus total value of the national expenditure

B   Total value of the national production less total value of the national expenditure

C   Total value of the national production multiplied by total value of the national expenditure

D   Total value of the national production which is the same as that of the national expenditure

5   **Which of the following constitute the income headings which make up the national income?**

A   Wages earned

B   Interest received

C   Rent and profit received

D   All of the above

6   **Which of the following make up the expenditure element of the national income?**

A   Gross consumption by firms and households

B   Investments made by individuals and firms

C   Both of the above

D   None of the above

7 **What is it that a nation must do to create and grow its national economy?**

A   Produce and sell goods and services

B   Spend money

C   Invest money

D   Sell to overseas buyers

8 **Saving is said to create a leakage from the otherwise 'perfect' system of the national economy. Which of the following best describes this effect?**

A   Saving money takes it out of the monetary system

B   Because the money is no longer available as part of the monetary system

C   Because an economist sees saving as any form of non-use of money, not saving in a bank

D   Because when money is not available for use, it cannot be part of the national income and expenditure cycle

9 **Which of the following best describes why taxation can be a leak on the national economy?**

A   Because the government takes money out of the system using taxation

B   Because money is removed from circulation from the moment of taxation until the government in turn spends it

C   Because taxation is inefficient and a 'sledge hammer' in terms of its effect on the economy

D   All of the above

10 **Which of the following best describes when taxation is not a drain on the national economy?**

A   When the government spends the taxation

B   When the government reduces taxation rates

C   When the government creates a new tax

D   When the government puts the tax back into the Bank of England

11 **Why is it that investment in equipment can have both a nil effect on the economy and be expansive, but is actually regarded entirely as the latter?**

A   Because it is too difficult to split

B   Because often it is both replacement and new capacity which is bought

C   Because spending stimulates the economy in any case so it is viewed as being expansive

D   All of the above

12 **Why is there a tendency for savings and investments to come together in the national economic cycle?**

A   Because one person's savings is another's investment

B   Because banks lend savings to those who want to invest

C   Because the two will always tend to balance each other out, as the economic cycle causes one to chase the other

D   Because savings and investments are the same thing

13 **Why is an estimate made of the consumption of capital in an economy?**

A Because it is important to know the figure involved so that arrangements can be made to create taxation to cover for it

B Because it provides a figure for true GNP, with depreciation written out

C Because it is a requirement of the European Union

D Because allowance needs to be made for this figure when calculating the money supply

14 **Why must national income be measured in real prices?**

A If they are not, then the market prices that it would include will not be correct

B The effect of inflation distorts the figures for national income

C National income has nothing to do with inflation

D It provides a constant and comparable measure

15 **Why is the promotion of capital investment important for the growth of an economy?**

A Because in general, the more equipment available, the more is produced and thus the more is sold

B Because it is important to keep a nation's capital equipment as modern and up to date as possible

C Because it will enable industry to make the most up to date goods which are usually the most saleable

D All of the above

Chapter 3 – Economic Trends and Management Policies

1 **In modern times reliance on non-intervention in markets has become discredited. Why?**

A   Because people tend to save when they can to protect themselves against difficult times which they perceive are coming or which have arrived

B   Because the world has changed so much since Victorian times

C   Because the national debt will never be repaid

D   Because the balance of payments since the second world war has always been in deficit

2 **In times of full employment, when demand is high and supply less strong, what is likely to happen?**

A   A revolution

B   Inflation

C   Deflation

D   High interest rates

3 **What is the difference between residual and seasonal unemployment?**

A   There is none

B   Residual is a term for those who can't or won't work, seasonal for those who don't have work due to temporary cyclical climatic driven lack of demand for employees

C   Residual is a term for those want to work but cannot find work, seasonal for those who only can find employment in the summer or at Christmas

D   Residual is a term used to describe those who have lost their jobs due to the failure of their firms, seasonal is used to describe those who are unemployed due to seasonal fluctuations in demand for employees

4 **Which of the following is untrue?**

A   Frictional unemployment is due to firms ceasing to trade

B   Frictional unemployment is solved by giving money to firms to keep people in employment

C   Frictional unemployment can be a good thing as it demonstrates increasing efficiency and the working of the market if it results in people moving from one job to another

D   Frictional unemployment can be solved by government action in bringing those so unemployed into contact with information about available jobs

5 **Which of the following is not a cause of structural unemployment?**

A   The employer becoming insolvent

B   Reduced demand for the good or service provided

C   Technological change

D   Overseas competition

6   **Why did the UK government encourage the opening of call-centres in the Dearn and Don valleys in south Yorkshire, which have given employment to many once employed in the coal and steel industries?**

A   To overcome structural unemployment

B   To encourage the development of new technology

C   To gain votes

D   To overcome frictional unemployment

7   **Gordon Brown famously once said 'We have broken the cycle of boom and bust'. Setting aside the political aspects, why did this receive so much derisive comment?**

A   You cannot break the cycle; it is the essence of a free market economy

B   Because the government created such a huge demand for borrowed funds to keep the UK going

C   Because the national debt was so large at the time

D   Because the IMF disagreed with him

8   **A slump or depression is characterised by**

A   High unemployment and low investment

B   High investment and low unemployment

C   Low employment and high investment

D   High government debt and low employment

9   **What term is used to describe an economy which is at full stretch, with high inflation, high wages and high interest rates?**

A   A boom

B   A recession

C   The accelerator effect

D   A cyclical turning point

10   **What is likely to happen when the demand for domestic and capital goods starts to drop off?**

A   It could be the start of a recession

B   Suppliers of such goods will invest ready to provide for the inevitable eventual increase in demand

C   It could be the start of an inflationary cycle

D   Research and development expenditure is likely to increase

11   **What is a recession?**

A   Two quarters in a year that show declining GDP

B   Two consecutive quarters in a year that show declining GDP

C   Two months in a year that show declining GDP

D   Two consecutive months in a year that show declining GDP

12 **An influential media economics commentator announces that she thinks that the economy is likely to go into a recession and repeats this several times over a couple of months. What is likely to happen?**

A The market for consumer durables and houses will show some signs of decline

B Nothing

C There will be a backlash and people will start spending

D A full scale recession will start

13 **Why is the maintenance of a high level of demand by government action not necessarily a good thing?**

A Because the government ought not to interfere with the free market

B Because it will create inflation

C Because it will create unemployment

D Because it interferes with the free market and may disguise or encourage activities which actually are of little or no value

14 **Keynesian economic management allows the government to some degree to turn it on and off to suit the stage of the cycle, sometimes creating the cycle. Which of the following is not caused as a result of such practices?**

A It destabilises the economy creating un-natural stop-go cycles

B It causes considerable government expenditure and high public employment

C It increases taxation to pay the for government's interventions

D It automatically brings in additional government revenues

15 **What does the term supply side mean in relation to monetarism?**

I The provision of enough goods and services to meet demands

II The provision of enough labour to meet demand

III The provision of tax cuts to make money available to spend and encourage people to work

IV Subsidies to failing industries

A I, II, III and IV

B II and III

C I and IV

D II and IV

Chapter 4 – Monetary Policy and Interest Rate Theories

1 **What is monetary policy?**

A The manipulation of interest rates and the supply of money to the economy

B The manipulation of the economy by the government

C The outcome of the decisions of the monetary policy committee

D The financial policy of the government

2 **Which of the following is not a purpose of monetary policy?**

A High and stable employment

B Low inflation

C Balanced balance of payments

D Low national debt

3 **Under a monetarist policy, if demand increases, prices remain more or less stable. Why?**

I   Because the supply of money is managed

II Because interest rates are managed

III Because free market forces are paramount

IV Because bank credit is managed

A None of the above

B All of the above

C I and III

D I, II and IV

4 **In a monetarist economy, why do prices remain stable when demand increases?**

A Because the government subsidises them

B Because output and employment increase in line with demand

C Because output and employment decrease in line with demand

D Because the government produces more money to cover up any price increase

5 **What role does the Monetary Policy Committee have?**

A To ensure that inflation does not exceed a specified level

B To ensure that prices remain stable in line with inflation

C To ensure that prices remain stable in line with the government's inflation target

D To ensure that inflation remains constant

6 **What restriction is placed upon the Monetary Policy Committee in relation to its setting of interests rates?**

A None

B It must act as the Chancellor of the Exchequer directs

C It must seek to maintain price stability, but within the government's economic policy

D Both B and C

7   In recent times, the 2% inflation target has received less attention by HM Treasury. Why is this?

A   Because to get the rate down to 2% would mean much higher interest rates, which would hamper economic growth

B   Because to get the rate down to 2% would be unrealistic in the short to medium term given the size of the national debt which needs to be serviced

C   Because it is expected that market forces will result in the inflation rate dropping

D   Because the government feels that voters are happier with a higher inflation rate rather than lower taxes

8   Why does a change in interest rates effect borrowers, lenders and savers?

A   Because lenders will be more keen to borrow as they will generate more income

B   Because potential borrowers will be more keen to save so income to lenders will decrease

C   Because savers will look for other places to put their money, so there will be less money to lend to borrowers

D   Because a shift will make borrowing, lending and saving either more or less attractive and either increase or decrease spending, with knock-on effects on the economy

9   Why does a change in interest rates affect the value of and demand for stocks and shares?

A   Because a shift in interest rates will make investments in these items more or less attractive to investors

B   Because their prices are automatically linked

C   Because people prefer to rely on guaranteed Bank of England rates than those paid by less safe corporates

D   Because if interest rates decline, fewer people will want to risk relying on corporates for dividends and coupon payments

10   What effect on prices does the exchange rate for sterling have?

A   A falling pound will reduce export prices thereby increasing inflation

B   A rising pound will reduce import prices thereby reducing inflation

C   A rising pound will increase import prices thereby increasing inflation

D   A falling pound will increase import prices thereby reducing inflation

11   What are open market operations?

A   Any transactions by the Bank of England that are made public

B   Any transactions on the stock market by the Bank of England that are made public

C   The purchase and sale of British Government securities by the Bank of England

D   The purchase and sale of blue chip securities by the Bank of England

12 **If the Bank of England wishes to prevent interest rates from rising what must it do?**

A Ensure that the Monetary Policy Committee makes the right decision

B It must stop gilts from falling in price because if they do, their yields will increase and to compete, the banks will have to raise interest rates to savers

C It must stop gilts from going up in price, because if they do, interest rates will rise too to match this in order to remain attractive to savers

D It must instruct the London Stock Exchange to increase the price of gilts so as to ensure that their yield falls in order to remain competitive with interest rates offered by banks

13 **By buying gilts, the Bank of England increases the market and therefore their value, whilst reducing their yield, so interest rates do not need to rise in competition with gilts. The purchase also has an inflationary effect, why?**

A Because the purchase is made by the Bank of England, it uses 'new' money and there is more money in circulation as a result

B Because the yield has gone down, or at least remained the same, so more money is needed for the same amount

C Because interest rates have gone down, or at least remained the same, so more money is needed for the same amount

D All of the above

14 **What are quantitative and qualitative directives?**

A Instructions from the Bank of England to the banks about the size and nature of their lending

B Instructions from the EU about the size and nature of domestic lending

C Instructions from HM Treasury which over-ride the statutory role of the Monetary Policy Committee to maintain inflation to a given percentage

D Instructions from HM Treasury to the banks about the size and nature of their lending

15 **What is the cash ratio?**

A The amount of cash to gold that the Bank of England is required to maintain under its Charter

B The amount of cash that the retail banks are required to retain in proportion to their lending

C The amount of cash and near cash equivalents that the retail banks are required to maintain in proportion to their lending

D The amount of cash in circulation in proportion to the gross domestic product or gold

Chapter 5 – Inflation and the Housing Market

1   What is inflation?

A   A rise in the value of money and a fall in the level of prices

B   A rise in the value of money and a rise in the level of prices

C   A drop in the value of money and drop in the level of prices

D   A fall in the value of money and a rise in the level of prices

2   What are the common factors of and differences between the Retail Price Index and the Consumer Price Index?

A   They each measure prices but RPI is all prices and CPI is only domestic ones

B   They each measure inflation but RPI is all inflation in the retail sector and CPI is domestic inflation only

C   CPI differs only from RPI in the actual calculation, the households measured and items included

D   They are the different names for the same thing

3   What is inflation likely to do to the value of a pension?

A   Increase it

B   Reduce it

C   Nothing

D   Make it stay the same

4   If inflation is a feature of an economy, which of the following will happen?

A   The real value of pensions will decrease and the real value of physical assets will increase

B   The real value of pensions will increase and so will that of physical assets

C   There is no correlation of real values of pensions to other assets so it cannot be said how they will relate to each other

D   The real value of pensions will decrease and without a stronger market for them, the real value of physical assets will also decrease

5   What might make inflation a good thing for an economy?

A   When it is low, it simply increases the money supply

B   It inhibits people from spending so they save more and provide money to the banks to lend

C   It can build in an added profit for producers who increase prices to match inflation if they can keep their costs down

D   There is never a time when inflation can do any good for an economy

6   Why might inflation lead to an imbalance in the balance of payments?

A Because prices within a country will go up and might rise more than those of competitor countries, which purchasers will choose as a consequence

B Because the exchange rate will deteriorate in line with inflation and make purchases more expensive

C Because worsening exchange rates and increasing prices will lead to higher import costs and fuel inflation further

D All of the above

7   Why do people with real assets tend to gain in inflationary times, whilst those whose assets are denominated in a fixed cash sum tend to lose?

A Because real assets increase in monetary terms, whilst financial assets being denominated in currency gets progressively worth less reduce in real terms

B Because real assets always increase in value faster than money

C Because property prices always increase in the long term

D The statement is not true and does not reflect the position with the two types of asset

8   Why do shares tend to increase in value in inflationary times?

A They don't

B Because they represent physical assets which increase in value in such times

C Because profits tend to increase due to the inflationary effect and make them more valuable in unit terms

D Both B and C

9   What is demand pull inflation?

A When demand in an economy is greater than supply, prices increase due to potential shortages

B When demand in an economy is less than supply, prices increase due to potential shortages

C When supply in an economy is greater than demand, prices increase due to potential shortages

D When supply in an economy is less than demand, prices decrease due to potential shortages

10   What is cost push inflation?

A When costs rise and thus prices increase to cover this rise

B When wages rise and thus prices rise to cover this rise

C When demand exceeds supply and prices rise

D When full employment makes wages rise and so prices rise

11   What is the underlying cause of inflation?

A Too much money in the economy

B Too little money in the economy

C Too high wages

D Too much demand

12   Why can government spending fuel inflation?

A   Because the government can more or less borrow at will and when it spends, often for political ends, this puts money into the economy

B   Because governments spend more than they have earned in taxes

C   Because the PSNB is larger than the GDP

D   Because the GDP is larger than the PSNB

13   If the government has a deficit, where is the surplus?

A   In the banks

B   In industry

C   In the private sector

D   Overseas

14   Why is it that if wage rises are linked to productivity cost push inflation might be solved?

A   Because people will work harder and have less time to spend

B   Because they will have more money to spend and demand will counter the increased costs

C   Because more will be made for the same cost so prices will not have to rise due to increased costs

D   Because the government will get more taxes

15   At times of deflation, why are interest rates cuts not very effective at stemming this problem?

A   Because rates are likely to be low already so cuts will not encourage spending as much as they would at a stable time

B   Because they will reduce the price of borrowing but that is not the main reason why prices are reducing

C   Because they discourage investment

D   Because they encourage investment

Chapter 6 – The International Money Markets and Banks

1 What are the roles of the various financial markets in the overall international money market?

A Making payments

B Settling debts

C Providing credit

D All of the above

2 What is the difference between a domestic and a foreign financial market?

A A domestic market is when all parties are within one country, a foreign market is when at least one party is in a different country from at least one of the other parties

B Any financial market located outside the UK is a foreign one, any within the UK is a domestic one

C Any financial market whose physical building is located in a country other than the UK

D Any financial market that provides services to customers who are located in either the UK or an overseas country

3 What is an external or eurocurrency market?

A A financial market which deals only in the euro or currencies used by EU members

B A financial market which deals in currencies that are not those of the country in which it is located

C A financial market located in any euro-using country

D A financial market located in any EU member country

4 Which of the following is a eurocurrency?

   I   The pound when dealt with in Paris

   II The euro dealt with in London

   III The euro dealt with in New York

   IV The euro dealt with in Luxembourg

A I and II

B I, II and III

C I, II, III and IV

D I and IV

5 Which of the following defines a eurodollar?

A A bank deposit held outside the USA

B A bank deposit with a time limit held outside the USA

C A bank deposit in euros held in the USA

D All of the above

6   What is the attraction of eurodollar deposits?

A   It is a method of keeping balances away from domestic tax authorities

B   A better rate of interest is available than domestic deposits

C   The interest rate is always paid gross, free of any taxation

D   All of the above

7   What is a Nostro account?

A   An account held by a foreign bank in an overseas country to settle international transactions

B   An account held in New York by a British bank

C   An account held in London by a New York based bank

D   All of the above

8   What is the main danger of the eurocurrency market worldwide?

A   That interest rates might fall

B   That interest rates might rise

C   That the market is not regulated

D   That the lending criteria are more relaxed and there is thus a danger of default

9   What is the real attraction of the eurocurrency market?

A   The complete deregulation of the market which is governed entirely by pure free market principles

B   That the market is not required to deal only in euros

C   That transactions can be done in secret

D   That it is free to use the market

10   Where is the eurocurrency market located?

A   London, New York and Frankfurt

B   New York, Singapore, London and Paris

C   London, New York, Singapore, Paris, Luxembourg, the Cayman Islands

D   It has no physical location

11   Why are Eurodollar interest rates closely related to domestic rates when there is no formal connection between the markets?

A   Because they are in competition with each other

B   Because banks borrow in the domestic market and lend in the eurocurrency market

C   Because banks borrow in the eurocurrency market and lend in the domestic one

D   All of the above

12   How is LIBOR calculated?

A   It is always quoted as 2/16th above the Bank of England base rate

B   It is a basket of the banks' transactions averaged by the BBA

C   It is set daily by the Federal Reserve

D   It is set daily by the Bank of England

13   What is a Certificate of Deposit?

A   A document entitling the holder to a sum of money which can be sold before maturity

B   A confirmation of a deposit

C   A certificate confirming that the holder has made a loan to the government

D   A certificate confirming that the holder is entitled to a sum of money from a UK bank

14   What is the share capital of a eurobank?

A   Its basic and permanent source of funding

B   The value of its capital on the London Stock Exchange

C   The nominal value of its capital

D   The number of shares issued by the bank

15   What is involved in asset-liability management?

A   The balancing of assets and liabilities in both size and time terms by banks

B   Ensuring that assets equal liabilities on the bank's balances sheet

C   Ensuring that the banks have enough cash to meet liabilities at all times

D   All of the above

Chapter 7 – International Loan and Bond Markets

1 **Which of the following are not a characteristic of a syndicated loan?**

A   It is made to governments by more than one bank

B   They involve more than one bank

C   They use one set of documentation and a managing agent

D   They always involve more than one bank

2 **Which of the following is an advantage to the borrower of a syndicated loan?**

A   They are cheaper than ones managed by one bank

B   Pound for pound they are usually faster than ones managed by one bank

C   They make foreign currency loans much easier to obtain

D   Because they involve governments, they are much safer than ones involving just a bank

3 **Which of the following is an advantage to a lending bank of being involved in a syndicated loan compared to a single lend?**

A   They are much safer due to the involvement of national governments

B   They enable banks to spread their risks

C   They bring in more in fees and interest

D   All of the above

4 **What is the manager's role in a syndicated loan?**

A   To co-ordinate the whole operation both in terms of lending and administration

B   To co-ordinate the administration as the lending decisions are up to the individual banks

C   To co-ordinate the lending as each bank will have its own administrative requirements

D   To ensure that costs are kept low

5 **Who usually provides most of the funds for a syndicated loan?**

A   The manager

B   The participating banks

C   Equally between the participating banks and the manager

D   The manager usually provides about a quarter with the remainder coming from the participating banks

6 **Which of the following is correct in relation to syndicated lending?**

A   Early repayments and cancellations are never permitted

B   Early repayments and cancellations are always permitted

C   Early repayments and cancellations are sometimes permitted

D   Early repayments and/or cancellations never attract a cost

7   Why is the contract to lend strongly biased in favour of a syndicated lender rather than the customer?

A   Because the loan is probably unsecured and therefore relatively risky for all the lenders

B   Because this is standard practice for all lending contracts

C   Because the customer is usually at a disadvantage in needing the money so has little choice other than to agree

D   All of the above

8   Why is there a clause in syndicated loan contracts which permits the lenders to use the New York prime rate rather than LIBOR?

A   To give routine flexibility to the lenders

B   To enable the lenders to choose the most beneficial rate

C   To enable the borrower to choose the most beneficial rate

D   In case the London market closes as a result of a disaster

9   What is the difference between a eurobond and a foreign bond?

A   A eurobond is issued in the EU, a foreign bond is issued in a country other than that of the purchaser

B   A eurobond is sold in an overseas market other than that of the seller and is denominated in a currency other than that of the market in which it is sold, whilst a foreign bond is sold by a borrower in the market of another country and is denominated in that currency

C   A eurobond is denominated in euros, a foreign bond in a currency other than that of the issuer

D   A eurobond is sold in any market other than one on the EU to non-EU buyers whilst a foreign bond is any bond sold to someone who is not of the same nationality as the seller

10   Who buys eurobonds?

A   Anyone with access to a stock exchange

B   Anyone outside the country of issue

C   Investment banks place them with purchasers

D   Retail banks

11   What is the yield of a bond?

A   It is the return in percentage terms, measured against the cost to the purchaser

B   The coupon stated on the certificate

C   The coupon divided by LIBOR as a percentage

D   The return which the bond pays as stated on the certificate

12   The involvement of institutional investors in the eurobond market has had several beneficial effects. Which one of these is listed below?

A   That the market is made cheaper to borrowers

B   That the market is made more lucrative to the banks

C   That the market has been able to make larger bond issues

D   All of the above

13 **What is the fundamental feature which distinguishes the Eurobond market from that of the eurocredit market?**

A   The eurobond market provides tradable securities but the eurocredit market simply provides an opportunity for investors to hold short term loans

B   One is traded within the EU, the other outside

C   The returns on the eurobond are certain, those on eurocredit is not

D   The returns on eurocredits are certain, those on Eurobonds are not

14 **What is the function of a eurobond underwriter?**

A   Covers the insurance risk of non-payment when the bond matures

B   Covers the risk of the bond issue not fully being taken up

C   Guarantees the price at which the bonds will sell when issued

D   Guarantees the price above a minimum level for those holders who wish to sell bonds after the initial offering

15 **Of the following, which is (are) the main risk factors in relation to any bond purchase?**

A   The political or regulatory risks of the country in which the bond is issued

B   The creditworthiness of the issuer of the bond

C   The industry sector in which the issuer sits

D   All of the above

Chapter 8 – International Banking Risk

1 **Why is the risk related to eurocurrency transactions so great in legal terms?**

A Because UK and/or English law does not apply in Europe

B Because these transactions are cross border and there is no legal enforcement possible across some such boundaries

C Because the US Federal Authorities will not enforce US law outside the USA

D All of the above

2 **Which of the following examples suggests that in some legal jurisdictions the law will support claims upon foreign banks outside that jurisdiction?**

A Sokoloff v National City Bank (1928) a US case where a Russian sued the surviving element of a Russian bank for the return of a deposit made to that bank in Russia before the revolution

B Coutts v Brown Lecky (1947) when the parent of a depositor contested the validity of a guarantee

C Devaynes v Noble (1812) when a depositor sued the surviving partners of a bank after the death of one partner

D Joachimson v Swiss Bank Corporation (1921) when the duty of a bank to repay to its customer's written order was established

3 **What is the implication of the so called 'Act of State Doctrine'**

A An international agreement between the US and UK to enforce the repayment of bank deposits between the two

B An international agreement between a number of countries to enforce the repayment of bank deposits between all of the parties

C A threat by the US and UK to use force against any country refusing to repay deposits to one of their nationals, originating in the UK's bombardment of Alexandria in the 1880s

D All of the above

4 **Whose law applies in the UK, when someone from another country which has frozen its currency operation to a third country tries to enforce this domestic rule?**

A English or Scottish law depending upon which part of the UK the deposit is located

B English law

C EU law

D Any and all of the above

5 **What was the significance of the decision in the Libyan Arab foreign bank case?**

A It made eurocurrency much safer by more or less removing jurisdiction risk

B It made the deposits of euros in the UK much safer due to support from the USA

C It removed entirely any risk of non-repayment of eurodollar deposits

D It made it much safer to deal with Libya if you were a UK or US national

6   What is a bond?

A   A guarantee

B   A document that promises performance

C   A document that guarantees repayment

D   A promise to pay a sum of money when or if a certain event happens

7   How do British banks, overall and in general, maintain protection from foreign exchange risk?

A   They insure

B   They are part of a protection scheme with the Bank of England

C   They are part of an international protection scheme operated by the Federal Reserve and the Bank of England

D   The try to ensure, so far as is reasonable and possible, equal exposures in any given currency in terms of both assets and liabilities

8   Why is the per capita real income such an important issue to consider when assessing the country and economic risks of dealing with a country?

A   Because governments fall when this measure falls and when this happens, rules can change

B   Because in an emerging economy, or less politically stable one, revolutions can be triggered by this

C   Because equality in wealth or poverty can often point to, at least, political stability

D   All of the above

9   What does a surplus on the balance of payments position suggest?

A   An ability to finance internal debt

B   An ability to finance foreign debt

C   Serious capital outflows

D   Potential problems servicing domestic debt

10   What does it mean if a country has a debt/service ratio of 150%?

A   That it can repay its overseas borrowings immediately and still have half as much again remaining in its foreign reserves

B   That it is short of repaying its overseas borrowings by 50% of their value

C   That it will need to function for a year and a half to raise enough money to repay its foreign borrowings

D   That its foreign borrowings are worth one and a half times its annual exports

11   Why is the level of foreign currency reserves important when assessing the country risk related to lending to or dealing with a foreign country?

A   Because they are the sums that a country has for use if all else fails to pay for imports.

B   Because it is the amount that a country has to pay its foreign debts

C   Because it is what provides support to failing importers

D   Because gold and foreign currency are often preferable to the currency of some countries

12 **Let's imagine that Ying Yong is a huge Far Eastern dictatorship and financial powerhouse. What are the dangers of doing business with it?**

A   Dictatorships have a historical habit of being overthrown and when they are, no-one knows what the political and thus economic outcomes may be

B   There may be a 'Ying Yong Spring' when the people rebel. No-one knows what might happen after such a revolution

C   There may be a demand for democracy that might be granted, this might lead to a very different government that could have significant economic impact, positive or negative

D   All of the above

13 **How can a bank reduce or avoid country risk when lending or dealing with a country?**

A   Diversify across a range of countries with different perceived levels of risks from different issues

B   Avoid lending too much to one or a group of countries with common characteristics

C   Only lend short term to perceived higher risk countries

D   All of the above

14 **Greece recently defaulted on its loans, but this was not reported as such in the media. How did it default?**

A   It restructured its debt, which is the same as defaulting

B   It failed to repay some of its debt, which is defaulting

C   It borrowed more to pay debt off, which amounts to the same thing

D   It was loaned money by the EU

15 **Why were the banks prepared to take a huge loss on Greek debt in the recent problems which the country experienced?**

A   Because it is better to be realistic and value the debt at what it is worth, rather than what it was worth

B   Because the EU insisted

C   Because there were significant domestic tax advantages for the banks if they did this

D   Because the EU promised that it would help the banks if they got into difficulties

Chapter 9 – Securitisation and Globalisation

1 What is securitisation of debt?

A The issue of bonds or notes to raise finance

B The selling of secured loans on the secured credit market

C The raising of finance by selling bonds to a secondary holder

D Selling negotiable notes at a discount

2 What is meant by the intermediation role of banks?

A Their ability to find buyers for bonds

B When banks have to help to sustain the economy of a specific industry sector by lending on bonds

C It describes their role of putting those with too much money in touch with those who do not have enough

D It describes their legal requirement to ensure that there is enough cash in certain parts of the country at any given time, working with the Bank of England

3 Why is it that bonds can be a cheaper way to borrow than bank finance?

A Because banks have to cover the cost of holding their liquidity ratios

B Because some very high rated borrowers can obtain bond finance at a risk premium below that of bank borrowing

C If a bank's credit rating falls, they cannot access funds as cheaply so have to pass on the costs to borrowers

D All of the above

4 How did the US trade deficit encourage the rise of securitised debt?

A The US had to raise funds to cover the deficit somehow and bonds were just one way

B Japan and Germany had large surpluses and borrowed on their capital markets using bonds

C Foreign investors were worried about putting money into US banks so lent it to companies by way of bonds instead

D All of the above

5 Given that banks, relatively speaking, were squeezed out of lending due to the rise of the bond market, how did they actually remain active with such instruments?

A They issued bonds themselves to retain their liquidity needs

B They invested in bonds issued by governments and corporates

C They sold bonds that they held to raise cash

D All of the above

6 How did the banks become even more deeply involved in securitisation of debt when bond issues failed?

A Because they had underwritten the bonds

B Because they bought the bonds that were not issued cheaply

C Because they lent money to the corporates whose note issues failed

D All of the above

7   What general features of the financial environment encouraged the expansion of securitisation?

A   Deregulation

B   Lower inflation and a willingness to accept lower returns for more stable prices of bonds

C   The IT revolution which made bond trading and dealing much easier and cheaper

D   All of the above

8   Why are securitised domestic mortgages (for example) said to be 'off balance sheet' items?

A   Because they do not appear on the balance sheet of their investors

B   Because the originating bank sells the mortgages and receives cash for them

C   Because the originating bank lends the SPV a proportion of the debt to make investing a more attractive proposition to the SPV's bondholders

D   All of the above

9   Why does the originating bank still have an interest in the loans sold to the SPV when it no longer owns them or the SPV?

A   Because it administers the loans and hopes to make a turn on the sum paid to it and the amount which it passes on to the SPV to cover the bond interest

B   Because there is always a recourse clause included in any SPV contract

C   Because it wants them to do well so that it can retain credibility for any future SPV sales

D   Because it has to show them in its accounts as a contingent liability

10   Why is it that the banks' one time hold on the lending market has been seriously eroded by the bond and securitisation process?

A   The availability of IT to enable bond investors to track performance and make their own assessments of bond issuers

B   The availability of IT to process everything fast

C   IT's ability to send e-mails

D   The removal by IT of the need for physical bond certificates

11   Relatively speaking, as banks took up securitised debt to replace loans that otherwise they would have provided, what happened to the risks that the banks incurred as a consequence?

A   Nothing, it is a simple exchange of one type of lending for another

B   They increased due to the potential price volatility of the underlying bonds

C   They reduced as bonds on the whole are more likely to be repaid by blue chip issuers than all a bank's lending book is to be repaid

D   All of the above

12   What undermined the customers' confidence in banks in 2008-9?

A   Their greed

B   Their incompetence

C   Their losses caused as a result of the collapse of the value of their securitised assets

D   Their inability to lend money

13 **What is Commercial Paper?**

A   Shares in a company

B   Stock in a company

C   Stocks or shares in a company

D   Short term promissory note sold by a company at a discount

14 **The secondary markets for non-USCP are more active than the primary and USCP. Why is this?**

A   They are not as technologically advanced

B   The US demands shorter term lending

C   Because there is a larger secondary market outside the US for commercial paper

D   Because they have a slightly longer maturity date than USCP

15 **What is euro-commercial paper?**

A   Short term promissory note issued in a currency other than that of the country of issue

B   CP which is issued in Europe at a discount

C   CP which is issued in Europe denominated in euros

D   CP which is issued in any currency but US$

Chapter 10 – Economic Monetary Union (EMU)

1 **Which of the following was the main objective of the EMS?**

A   To create a political union

B   To make it easier to travel around the EU

C   To stabilise exchange rates across EU countries

D   To make things economically easier for the weaker countries

2 **The ERM did not work perfectly. As a result the Euro was established. Why did the ERM not work?**

A   Speculation which sent rates outside the agreed parameters

B   It was rigged

C   The UK withdrew

D   All of the above

3 **Under which treaty was the euro and the European Central Bank created?**

A   The Lisbon Treaty

B   The London Treaty

C   The Treaty of Rome

D   The Maastricht Treaty

4 **Which of the following are the basic principal(s) of the euro's fiscal policy?**

A   No excessive budget deficits

B   No monetary financing of budget deficits

C   No bail outs of bankrupt governments

D   All of the above

5 **What destroyed the Latin Currency Union of the 19th Century?**

A   War between the members

B   War between the members and neighbours

C   Large budget deficits and the creation of false money in Italy and Greece

D   All of the above

6 **What was ERM2 designed for?**

A   A replacement for ERM 1

B   A way to make ERM work when ERM 1 had failed

C   A means of admitting less strong new states to the euro

D   To fiddle the entry requirements so that more or less any nation could join ERM

7 **Which of the following countries joined the euro without their economies meeting the convergence criteria?**

A   France

B   Germany

C   The Netherlands

D   Greece

8 **Why did the euro not eliminate exchange rate risk?**

A   Because there are other currencies to consider besides the euro

B   Because people do not trust it so try to use other currencies

C   Because not all countries in the EU us it

D   Because most trade is in US dollars and sterling

9 **Price stability was a promised euro benefit. Why did this not happen in many parts of the EU?**

A   Because wages went up

B   Because money supply increased with cheap credit associated with the euro

C   Because demand failed

D   Because supply failed

10 **Why did the anticipated elimination of budgetary deficits not only not happen, but actually grew?**

A   The availability of cheap money to governments

B   Failed tax systems that did not collect money

C   Inflation continued despite suggestions that the euro would stop it

D   All of the above

11 **Why has the euro not become a reserve currency?**

A   Because it is so unreliable that few have long term faith in it

B   Because trade carried on in the main in US dollars

C   Because of the inflation that attacked the peripheral countries particularly after the 2008 crash

D   All of the above

12 **What does it mean to a sovereign country to lose the ability to set its exchange rates?**

A   The surrendering of its gold and currency reserves to the central authority

B   An inability to manage the domestic economy by manipulation of exchange rates

C   A loss of international prestige

D   All of the above

13   **Other than the United Kingdom which is the largest and longest surviving free trade area in the world?**

A   Australia

B   China

C   The EU member states

D   The Vatican

14   **What is the over whelming characteristic of the economies of the ten nations that are EU members, which are not members of the euro?**

A   Inflation

B   Deflation

C   Cheap money

D   A large fiscal deficit, beyond that permitted by the euro convergence criteria

15   **Why was the stability and growth pact suspended in 2003?**

A   Because it did not work

B   Because it was too successful and encouraged inflation

C   Because Germany and France broke it and refused to pay the fines that a breach required

D   Because it prevented weaker countries entering the euro

Chapter 11 – Public Finance

1   What two main purposes is public finance raised for?

A   Defence and education

B   Control the economy and provide for government cash shortfalls

C   Provision of government services and re-distribution of wealth

D   All of the above

2   What are taxes?

A   An unnecessary and unpopular burden

B   Compulsory payments to the government

C   Unavoidable

D   All of the above

3   In relation to indirect taxation, why can the yield be quickly increased if demand for a product in inelastic?

A   Because the state simply increases the rate of taxation on the product

B   Because the more that is bought, the more tax will come in

C   Because the less that is bought, the more tax will come in

D   Because the state can decrease the rate of taxation on the product and increase the demand

4   What is a progressive tax?

A   One which incorporates new ideas

B   One which taxes relatively rich people less than relatively poor people

C   One which places the larger proportional burden on the better paid

D   One which places the smaller proportional burden on the better paid

5   What is meant by the taxable capacity of a nation?

A   Its people's and organisations' ability to pay

B   The GDP of a nation

C   The total National Income

D   The figure of taxation at which the national income will start to drop

6   What type of tax is UK Income Tax?

A   Progressive

B   Regressive

C   PAYE

D   Structured

7   What is the difference between marginal and average tax rate?

A   Marginal is charged only to low earners, average is across the board on all income

B   Marginal is the rate applied to each slice of income, average is the overall rate per payer

C   Marginal is the rate applied to all income, average is the rate applied to each slice of income

D   Average is charged only to low earners, marginal to all earners

8 Which of the following assets are not subject to Capital Gains Tax?

A The home of the taxpayer

B A vintage car

C Stocks and shares

D A holiday home

9 Why is VAT regressive?

A Because the rate reduces depending on the item or service purchased

B Because the burden is the same regardless of who pays it

C Because it hits poor people in addition to rich people

D All of the above

10 Why is smuggling a potential tax problem?

A Because it is illegal

B Because it reduces prices

C Because it provides tax free goods

D All of the above

11 What is likely to happen if there is a move from direct to indirect taxation?

A Inflation will occur

B Deflation will occur

C People will save more

D People will spend more

12 Which of the following is not a traditional activity for the provision of public services?

A Defence

B Transport

C Car manufacturing

D Governance costs

13 What are merit goods and/or services?

A Things which provide personal benefits

B Things which provide personal benefits but which are provided to those in need or want at free or reduced cost by government expenditure

C Things which provide personal benefits but which are never going to be provided by government expenditure

D Things which people choose to buy on their own account regardless of whether there is a government provided free or reduced cost alternative

14 **Transfer payments using taxation move money from some groups of taxpayers to other groups of people in the country. What will the effect of this be?**

A It will increase demand

B It will change the pattern of demand

C It will not change demand

D It will decrease demand

15 **What is a structural budget deficit?**

A A serious overspend by the government

B A lack of taxation income

C The share of the deficit that cannot be covered in repayment terms when an economy is at its normal levels of activity

D A shortage of public cash

Chapter 12 – Financial Crisis 2007 – 2009

1   Which of the following were causes of the 2007-9 financial crisis?

A   The production of new financial instruments which were difficult to understand

B   Political over emphasis on home ownership

C   Packaging up and selling loans worldwide

D   All of the above

2   What was the consequence for original lenders of their production of asset backed securities?

A   Creation of risk free lending

B   Encouragement of sub-prime lending by secondary lenders

C   Encouragement to the originators of lending without reference to basic rules of lending

D   Access to the prime market to sub prime lenders

3   Which of the following were interdependent factors which triggered the US property crash?

I   Lending to people whose ability to repay depended largly on ever increasing house prices

II   Over-optimistic assumptions about house price inflation

III   Self certification of income by borrowers

IV   Self certification of employment situation by borrowers

A   None of the above

B   All of the above

C   I and II

D   III and IV

4   How did the so called sub-prime and toxic debts get into the world banking system?

A   The US banks planted them

B   They were bought and traded by banks worldwide

C   Both A and B

D   Monoline insurers who promised to cover the value of the securitised debt sold them

5   When an economic bubble effect bursts why does it become difficult or impossible to diversify risk associated with the bubble?

A   It is not so, risks can continue fully to be diversified

B   Because the fashion for that risk is exhausted

C   Because no-one or increasingly fewer buyers are available to take on the risk

D   All of the above

6   Why did LIBOR rise sharply when it became apparent that Bear Stearns might not be able to meet its commitments?

A   Because LIBOR is the rate at which banks lend to each other

B   Because no-one trusts banks

C   Because LIBOR includes a risk premium and this became very high to cover the risk of default

D   All of the above

7   Why is it important to ensure that when a bank uses Lender of Last Resort facilities, this is kept quiet?

A   Because if one use them, all the others will want them

B   Because on the whole, no-one knows what it means and it is best not to let them know

C   Because it is a last resort for banks that are unable to obtain finance elsewhere and suggests that they are in serious trouble

D   Because it might put pressure on the Bank of England to increase interest rates

8   Why did the takeover of Bear Stearns by J P Morgan provoke a further decline in confidence in the banking system of the world?

A   Because Bear Stearns was very popular

B   Because J P Morgan was not popular

C   Because Northern Rock had just been nationalised

D   Because it suggested that Bear Stearns, a huge player, was worthless

9   Why did Leman's inability to renew wholesale funding bring about its collapse?

A   Because it relied on the money markets for funding rather than depositors and shareholders

B   Because LIBOR was too expensive for it

C   Because Bear Stearns had just been taken over by J P Morgan

D   Because its share price had just collapsed

10   Why did the crisis spread to the extent that working capital provision for bank customers became difficult to obtain?

A   Because banks thought that many of their customers had shares in defaulting banks

B   Because banks needed to retain what liquidity they had to keep themselves afloat

C   Because banks dare not risk liquidity on any other than the safest of loans

D   Both B and C

11   Why did the US and UK Governments cut taxes?

A   Because they needed to encourage their economies by giving potential spenders the ability to spend more

B   Because their national debts were so low due to inflation created by the crash

C   Because their national debts were so high but interests rates had fallen so they did not need so much to service them

D   All of the above

12   How did the HM Government become a major shareholder in the banks in the UK?

A   No-one would buy their shares, so the government did

B   The shares crashed in value so the government bought them as a cheap long term investment

C   The banks needed cash for liquidity and no-one would buy any new shares so the government bought new ordinary and preference shares in huge amounts

D   They had to take shares in lieu of cash for taxes

13   What is quantitative easing?

A   Printing money

B   Buying any asset from a bank to release money to it

C   Buying buildings from banks to release money to it

D   Buying mostly gilts from a bank to release money to it

14   HM The Queen asked why the signs of the crash were not noticed. No-one gave her a full answer. Why were they not noticed?

A   No-one likes to hear bad news that appears to buck a trend

B   It might have imperilled the large bonus culture

C   The leaders of the banks were not people with professional qualifications

D   All of the above

15   Why has history so much to teach us about financial crisis?

A   Because something like this has happened before

B   Because of the South Sea Bubble

C   Because of Overend & Gurney and the City of Glasgow Bank collapses

D   All of the above

Chapter 13 – Bank Regulation

1 **Of the following, which are not required characteristics for an organisation to be authorised to be a bank?**

A   That managerial staff hold professional banking qualifications

B   That the bank be run by fit and proper people

C   That the bank has a business plan

D   That the bank has sound systems and controls

2 **Why are banks regulated?**

A   To try to ensure that the deposits made by the public are as secure as possible

B   To ensure that the money supply is under control

C   Because if they were not, there is a good chance that they would take unnecessary risks

D   All of the above

3 **It is recognised now that banks are vulnerable to failure because of the financial structure which is displayed in their balance sheets. What is the most likely reason for this vulnerability?**

A   Because they might be short of cash

B   Because banks are highly geared

C   Because banks are highly geared and rely on short term deposits

D   Because banks rely on short term deposits

4 **Most banks assets are made up of long term loans. They tend not be readily saleable in times of need which is a threat to the bank's liquidity. If such a loan goes bad, what will be the effect on the bank's capital?**

A   It will reduce by the amount that has to be written off

B   It will increase by the amount that has to be written off

C   Nothing

D   The value of the bank's shares will go down

5 **What is the main aim of prudential regulation and control?**

A   To stabilise the banking system

B   To limit damage to depositors

C   To limit damage to depositors and stabilise the banking system

D   To provide lender of last resort facilities

6 **What is the moral hazard that is created when banks are subject to Prudential controls?**

A   People trust them implicitly and fail to take reasonable personal care in choosing what do to do and how to deal with banks

B   Banks take excessive risks relying on the regulator to give a warning if they stray too far

C   Both A and B

D   That people will rely on the government to pay them for any losses

7   What is the 'too big to fail doctrine'?

A   That an overconfident large bank will rely on the government to bail it out if it makes too many mistakes

B   That the public will rely on the government to bail out a failing bank

C   That customers who are high net worth individuals rely on their financial power to ensure that the bank they are with does not fail

D   All of the above

8   How does regulation ensure liquidity adequacy?

A   It makes it a criminal offence to have insufficient liquidity in a bank

B   It defines suitable assets and sets minimum ratios

C   It sets minimum ratios for cash to assets

D   All of the above

9   What do the capital adequacy rules seek to achieve?

A   That depositors will be paid out if the bank fails

B   That there will be sufficient capital to absorb any losses

C   Provides a minimum ratio of capital to assets

D   Puts limits on the size of loans that a bank can make

10   In addition to acting as a buffer for any losses, which of the following does capital serve in a bank?

A   Provides the basic funds that the bank has to lend

B   Working capital

C   Maintain confidence

D   All of the above

11   What was the immediate effect of the Basle II Accord?

A   It made the competitive situation much more equal for both well and undercapitalised banks

B   It made capital adequacy ratios unachievable

C   It made liquidity ratios achievable

D   It ensured that the world banking system would remain solvent

12   If a bank breaches the Basle II Accord in terms of the ratio between capital and risk assets, what are the consequences?

A   It will have to increase its capital

B   It will have to sell more shares

C   It will have to sell some assets

D   All of the above

13 **Who sets the capital adequacy ratio for individual banks?**

A   The Basle II Accord Secretariat

B   The Central Bank of the country concerned

C   The regulator of the Country concerned

D   The World Bank

14 **Why does the banks' quest for profit conflict with the need for liquidity?**

A   Because the most profitable loans tend to be the least liquid

B   Because cash is tied up in loans for a long while

C   Because profits are not always cash

D   All of the above

15 **Why has it been recommended that banks ring fence their retail activities from those of any associated investment banking operation?**

A   It hasn't been recommended

B   Because the banks might use retail customers' deposits to indulge in risky transactions

C   Because the banks are too big

D   Because they need to pay out dividends

Chapter 14 – Banking/Financial Environment

1 **Banks have in the last few years been forced to reconsider the whole nature of their operations. Which of the following have triggered this fundamental review?**

A Income and cost pressures

B The financial crisis

C Failed lending policies and practices

D All of the above

2 **Why is that the more financially active an individual, the more they tend to demand banking and related services?**

A Because someone has to look after an ever-increasing amount of money

B Because their increased financial activities need to be serviced

C Because advertising makes them demand such services

D All of the above

3 **Why was the political decision taken to free the banks to provide additional and wider services, beyond those of the traditional retail bank?**

A To encourage their growth

B To encourage competition

C To create a market rather than an operationally-orientated framework for financial services

D All of the above

4 **Why did customer loyalty to banks decline as competition grew?**

A Customers placed value for money before loyalty

B Some banks could not provide the services that customers needed

C Customers disliked banks and were glad of a chance to vote with their feet

D Customers were not concerned with integrity, just cheapness

5 **Why did property lending cause the banks problems in the 1990s?**

A Excessive competition lead to risker lending with lower interest rates

B Excessive government regulation

C Not enough government regulation

D The US sub-prime lending collapse

6 **What was it about the general environment that caused banks and other financial institutions to continually review their operations and strategies in the period leading up to 2008?**

A Technology

B Deregulation

C Developments in the method of conducting business, e.g. securitisation

D All of the above

7 **The pressure to increase income resulted in the banks pulling back from low margin business. Into what did they move to replace this?**

A   Anything that made money

B   Personal business of any sort but in particular mortgage lending and charging for previously free services

C   Overseas lending

D   Lending to the government

8 **The banks reduction of staff to save costs was a double-edged sword. Why?**

A   Because there was no-one left to run the banks

B   Because they had to pay out huge sums in compensation to departing staff

C   Because the remaining staff had to be trained and/or retrained at huge cost

D   All of the above

9 **Why did UK banks tend to amalgamate in the period up to 2008?**

A   They had to make huge IT investments and it meant that there would be economies of scale

B   There was a need for a large number of customers once the IT had been installed as it tended to have a lot of spare capacity

C   They could reduce the number of branches and cut costs

D   All of the above

10 **Why does the concentration on IT and the loss of branches result in the increase in disloyalty of customers to their bank?**

A   Because there is no point of contact for them to approach should they need it

B   Because there is no-one with whom they can identify if they need to

C   Because banks are usually accessed by telephone or computer and this means that people have no sense of personal attachment

D   All of the above

11 **What is likely to happen to the face of the UK banking industry in the next few years?**

A   There will be more banks due to disposals of branches

B   There will be more opportunities for bank staff to shop around for employers who will be seeking their experience and skills

C   Customers will have more choice across a wider range of providers

D   All of the above

12 **Why is it that the pool of rental home occupiers is likely to decline in the future?**

A   Because fewer people will be able to afford to buy a house

B   Because more people will be able to buy a house

C   Because so many people already own a house, there will be less people who want to buy one

D   All of the above

13   **The 1986 Building Societies Act freed the societies to do more and wider business than just mortgage and allied lending to personal customers. What was the effect on some of the smaller societies?**

A   They took too many risks to boost their earnings

B   They encountered a skills shortage

C   They were swamped with business

D   They had to spend excessive amounts on new systems

14   **What do building societies exist to do?**

A   Lend money

B   Serve customers and their local communities

C   Make as much money as possible

D   Take on bottom end lending

15   **What is a private bank?**

A   A bank owned by its customers

B   A bank which is used only by a small group of customers who own it

C   A bank which provides retail and specialist personal services to high net worth customers

D   A bank which is owned by one family

Chapter 15 – Innovation and Technology in Banking

1   What is a so-called expert system?

A   A computer driven operation that replaces a number of highly skilled staff

B   A computer driven system that is written by experts

C   Any IT system that is written by experts

D   Any IT system that replaces experts

2   What has been a significant but unanticipated side-effect of the growing introduction of IT in banking?

A   That the banks saved money through the sheer amount of transactions that could be automated

B   That transaction for transaction there is much less employment in the banking industry today than when banking was entirely branch based

C   That the customer perception of banking is much more remote and impersonal due to lack of human contact

D   All of the above

3   Which of the following functions can an ATM perform?

A   Granting secured loan

B   Opening an account

C   Closing an account

D   Paying bills

4   What is the big difference between telephone and PC banking as a delivery channel?

A   The visualisation of the activities undertaken

B   The customer does not have to speak to someone

C   Telephones are much cheaper to answer than the provision of PC-based banking

D   All of the above

5   Why is it that banks that are not based around the provision of services using branches able to offer cheaper services and sometimes better rates of interest than traditional banks?

A   Because they rely on volume business

B   Because they can access funding more cheaply

C   Because their costs are lower

D   All of the above

6   Why do banks record telephone calls with customers?

A   Security

B   Training purposes

C   In case of subsequent disputes

D   All of the above

7 What is achieved by CTI?

A Linking telephone and computer technology so that they work together

B Simple ATM operation for the customer

C Cheaper ATM operation for the bank

D All of the above

8 What is a so-called clicks and mortar bank?

A Any type of retail bank for the mass market

B A high street bank that is operated using in-house ATMs rather than staff

C A PC-based banking service

D A bank that provides both IT and branch based banking

9 Which of the following inhibit customers from using IT based banking?

A Worries about security

B Lack of a PC

C Lack of instant response at busy times

D All of the above

10 Why do banks like internet banking so much?

A It is very cheap and makes banking a much more profitable operation than traditional methods

B It allows huge market penetration without the need for a traditional branch networks

C It keeps staff numbers relatively low

D All of the above

11 How do customers access mobile telephone delivery of banking services?

A By calling their branch

B By calling a call centre

C By downloading an APP

D Using an ATM

12 How do some telephones have the potential to replace cash?

A By having a swipe facility so that money can be downloaded at a till

B By accessing ATMs

C By telling the bank to send money to a creditor

D By advising a creditor that they can set up a direct debit

13 Why are branch banks in a vortex of decline?

A Because few people use them

B Because they are difficult to access

C Because as simpler and easier ways of accessing services arise there is less need to visit a branch and therefore less justification for having them

D All of the above

14 **Why do banks leave branches open when it is much cheaper to provide internet banking?**

A   Well sited branches remain a good source of income

B   They keep the bank's name in the public eye

C   They are liked and used by a large enough number of customers to warrant them staying open

D   All of the above

15 **In the context of granting a loan, why can an expert system never entirely replace the need for people?**

A   Because such systems lack subjective judgement

B   Because such systems are very impersonal

C   Because they treat applicants as numbers

D   Because people prefer to deal with people

ANSWER BANK

Chapter 1 – Financial Assets, Liabilities and Intermediaries

1   **B**   Because the two are so interconnected, it is impossible to understand one without the other

2   **D**   The sheet shows the position for the whole country. Therefore, someone who owes money in the country, must owe it to someone else. Therefore each asset is also a liability within the country and each liability also an asset.

3   **B**   It is never popular to raise taxes, so governments tend to run at a deficit, relying on their ability to borrow for the shortfall, hence the deficit.

4   **D**   Financial intermediaries put those with excess funds into contact with those who have a shortage, but they can only do this due to their knowledge and experience and the systems that they operate.

5   **C**   A financial intermediary takes financial assets from those who have more than they require in the immediate future and makes them available to those who do not have enough.

6   **D**   Financial intermediaries rely on incurring financial liabilities to raise funds. When these have been raised by way of deposits, the cash that has been deposited is then lent on and becomes a loan by the intermediary, which is a financial asset owned by the intermediary.

7   **D**   The underlying reason is that they believe that they will get the asset returned by the intermediary and that it will be less risky placing it with them rather than keeping it themselves. The prospect of a financial return, or the minimisation of loss, is usually an additional factor.

8   **B**   The sums which banks incur as liabilities, aggregated, are huge and give them very substantial sums to lend when required.

9   **D**   Their only resources would be their cash, any other monetary balances and physical assets. They could use the former by running them down partially or entirely, and/or turning assets into cash to fund their financial needs.

10   **A**   Banks are so large (or need to be large) that the effect of so many people making deposits and not instantly withdrawing their funds is, in effect, the same as one person depositing their funds for a long period.

11   **C**   They can be used in more or less the same way as notes and coins and therefore although they do not physically exist, they can be used as money and are counted as such.

12   **B**   Banks create money by making credit available to customers through loans and overdrafts which are, in effect, artificial money that works in exactly the same way as the customer depositing their own funds into the account, in terms of its effect when spent.

13   **D**   They all impact on money supply.

14   **A**   Loans to any other than short dated British government stock are not included.

15   **A**   The multiplier can only work if there is some cash in the system to start with. Its lending then causes the money in the system to grow as credit is provided.

Chapter 2 – National Income

1 **D** The measurement of national consumption is measured in the main by the consumption of all goods by households.

2 **B** National production is measured by the amount of economic production by firms.

3 **C** National income is made up of the amount which individuals in the economy earn from doing their work plus the income that goes to those people and organisations which own the factors of production, these being land and capital.

4 **D** Production, expenditure and income within a national economy must all equal the same sum.

5 **D** The national income is made up of all of the four headings.

6 **C** The expenditure element of a national economy can only be made up of all expenses incurred by both households and firms.

7 **A** The only way that income can be produced is by the sale of goods and services. It does not matter who buys them, but without them, no-one will pay the people and firms in a country any money, so the economy will stagnate or reduce in size.

8 **D** Savings are only part of the system when they are made available to monetary intermediaries. If money is simply held back (usually in the form of cash, but also for example as an unpresented cheque) then the multiplier effect cannot happen, nor can anything happen as a result of it being spent. Therefore saving in this sense withdraws funds from an economy and is in effect, a leakage.

The others have elements of truth and correctness, but it is only when funds are actually withdrawn from the system entirely that savings act as a leak on the economy.

9 **B** Taxation only removes money from an economy up to the point where the government retains it. Once it spends it, then it is released back into the economy.

10 **A** The money that is tax goes back into circulation when the government uses it to buy something, or gives it away as benefits.

11 **C** All are correct in one way or another, although none is correct by itself.

12 **C** If savings are less than investment (which includes the stock of finished goods), then people will have the ability to buy more than is made. As a result, producers will find it relatively easier to sell goods so will make more which will make investment converge towards saving. The opposite also applies, so investment will converge towards savings, or vice versa although it might take some time for the convergence to be appreciated.

13 **B** The Gross National Product figure would not be correct (or as correct as it is possible to arrive at) if the amount of 'irrecoverable' capital that had been used in the period was not allowed for. This figure is that allocated to depreciation and needs to be deducted from GNP, otherwise GNP would be like a firm's profit figure that included depreciation and therefore seriously flawed.

14 **D** Real rather than market prices enable a real measure to be provided, otherwise the figures would be distorted by inflation and not be comparable.

15   **A**   Generally speaking and given an adequate labour force, the more capital equipment is available, the more will be made, the more sold and the more income obtained.

Chapter 3 – Economic Trends and Management Policies

1   **A**   Simply leaving the market to sort out imbalances in demand and supply has been shown not always to work, at least in the short term, although it might do on occasions. This is why governments sometimes intervene in markets to stimulate them.

2   **B**   Inflation is caused by too much demand chasing too few goods. This results in prices increasing.

3   **B**   Residual refers to those who are more or less long term unemployed, either because they cannot or will not work. Seasonal is a term used to describe unemployment which is attributable to reduced demand for employment at particular times of year such as in the tourist industry in the UK, which tends to employ fewer people in the Winter than the Summer.

4   **B**   Giving money to firms might be a very short term solution to frictional unemployment, but it is merely papering over the cracks. If a firm is insolvent in the long term, employment subsidies will not keep it going.

5   **A**   This is frictional unemployment.

6   **A**   Structural unemployment arose due to the loss of the coal and steel industries. The creation of call centres was a deliberate ploy to try to create long term jobs to overcome this.

7   **A**   A free market economy has and always will operate on a cyclical basis, i.e. the so called boom and bust.

8   **A**   High unemployment and low investment.

9   **A**   These events are all highly characteristic of a boom at its height.

10   **A**   It is likely to be an early sign of the start of a recession.

11   **B**   The official UK description of a recession is when two consecutive quarters in a year show declining GDP.

12   **A**   It is likely that due to the effect on the collective confidence of the nation, if enough and sufficiently credible people say that things are going to get worse, they probably will do. The first sign is often the slowing down of the housing market.

13   **D**   Such government interference may be a good thing to stimulate demand when this is needed, but it can equally be a bad thing, which helps industries or specific businesses to produce goods and services that are not really needed or actually in demand. It can thus distort the economy and even hide 'lame ducks' through subsidies.

14   **D**   Additional government revenues are not an automatic result of employing Keynesian techniques, but they may happen if higher consumption occurs on taxed items, or if additional taxation has to be levied to pay for government interventions.

15   **B**   Supply here refers to incentives to work and ensuring that there is enough labour to meet demands. It is not so much ensuring that goods are there, as ensuring that the things which fulfil demand are available or the things which inhibit supply are reduced so far as is possible.

Chapter 4 – Monetary Policy and Interest Rate Theories

1   **A**   The manipulation of interest rates and the supply of money to the economy.

2   **D**   Low national debt is not a direct objective of monetary policy, although it may be a by-product.

3   **D**   The factors in I, II and IV, individually or collectively are managed under a monetarist policy which, in theory, should prevent excessive price rises when demand increases.

4   **B**   If output and employment increase in line with demand, then prices ought to remain more or less stable.

5   **C**   Its aim is to try to maintain prices and to do this, the government sets an inflation target, advised by the Committee via the Governor of the Bank of England. The stability will be within that target.

6   **C**   Its only restriction is that its prime function is to maintain price stability, but this must be done within the prevailing governmental economic policy.

7   **A**   Interest rates would have to rise to get inflation to meet the target and since the 2008 banking crash, when the base rate has only been 0.5%, this would mean a significant rise and hamper prospects of economic growth.

8   **D**   A shift either way will influence all three groups to do more of what they do, or less with consequent effects on the economy.

9   **A**   Although there is no automatic link a move in interest rates either way, this will mean that stocks and shares become either more or less attractive in terms of their yields, thus the market will change depending upon interest rates.

10   **B**   If the pound increases in value relative to other currencies, import prices will decrease as UK importers have to pay less in foreign currencies for the same amount of goods. This will result in prices falling and have the same effect on inflation.

11   **C**   The Bank of England buying and selling gilts is known as open market operations.

12   **B**   If gilts fall, the yield will increase and so they will become more attractive as investments than putting money in the bank. The banks will have to increase interest rates to savers in turn to remain attractive (and to borrowers to pay for this). Therefore, the bank must maintain the price of gilts.

13   **A**   The Bank of England purchases use new money, thus the money supply is increased by the purchases. More money in circulation means higher inflation. Settlement of the gilts is done by cheques drawn on the Bank of England so whether banks buy them or not, they get the money to lend as the cheques are deposited into bank accounts in the retail system. This makes more money available for banks to lend and that in turn increases the inflationary effect.

14   **A**   The Bank of England issues these directives from time to time, regarding how much the banks may lend and what form it may take.

15   **B**   The banks are required to maintain 0.15% of their eligible liabilities as cash at the Bank of England.

Chapter 5 – Inflation and the Housing Market

1   **D**   Inflation happens when unit for unit, more money is required to buy the same unit of goods.

2   **C**   They are very similar, but are calculated slightly differently and include different items.

3   **B**   Reduce it if it is a fixed sum because inflation makes any unit of money worth less over time.

4   **D**   Inflation decreases the unit value of everything, but if demand increases for any assets, then the consequent increase in its value might exceed the increase in price which is caused by inflation.

5   **C**   Producers who are able to keep their costs down can increase prices in line with inflation and make more profit.

6   **D**   All of these factors will lead to an increase in any imbalance in the balance of payments.

7   **A**   Real property prices tend to increase to compensate for inflation, but many financial assets being denominated in cash terms, stay the same size so the capital invested reduces in value.

8   **D**   Both B and C are correct due to the pressure of inflation to increase profits and asset values.

9   **D**   Demand pull inflation is when there is too much demand being made for too few goods, so prices rise.

10   **A**   When any costs rise and this is passed on customers via increased prices.

11   **A**   The underlying thing which triggers inflation is the availability of too much money in the economy. Demand pull can only happen if there is money to feed it. Cost push can only happen if there is money to pay the higher prices that are demanded.

12   **A**   Governments are under pressure to provide bigger and better services whilst collecting fewer taxes. This puts more money into an economy and fuels inflation.

13   **C**   The surplus must be in the private sector, stored in many places, but often in the banks.

14   **C**   More will be made for the same wage costs, so there will be no need to increase prices.

15   **B**   Deflation happens not because of a lack of stimulus as interest rates will already below.

Chapter 6 – The International Money Markets and Banks

1   **D**   The various financial markets provide the same services in the field of international finance as do the domestic banks within the UK. They transfer money, settle debts and provide credit.

2   **A**   Where at least one of the parties is in a different country from at least one of the others.

3   **B**   Any financial market which deals with currencies other than that of the country in which it is located is a eurocurrency market, regardless of which currencies it deals with.

4   **B**   A eurocurrency is any dealing in a currency when it is dealt with in a market outside that of its country of domicile.

5   **B**   A eurodollar deposit is simply a bank deposit of US dollars held outside the USA with some form of time limitation to the deposit.

6   **B**   A better rate of interest is always available on deposits due to the relaxation of liquidity requirements by the domestic authorities.

7   **D**   A Nostro account is any account held by an overseas bank in a foreign country for the purposes of settling its international transactions in that country.

8   **C**   The market is not regulated at all as the deposits are in currencies other than those of the country of domicile and are held by non-nationals.

9   **A**   The absence of any regulation is the over-riding attractive factor.

10   **D**   The market is a virtual one. There is no building, but it is created by vast numbers of telephone and electronic communications between the participants around the world.

11   **A**   They are inevitably linked as all interest rates are in competition with each other. The lack of a formal link is a technical one; regardless of this, market forces are bound to result in competition which will lead to movements which relate to each other.

12   **B**   it is an average calculation by the BBA of the previous day's transactions by a panel of at least eight banks of high repute in London.

13   **A**   It is simply a wholly negotiable document which confirms the deposit of a sum of money with a bank which can be sold at any time up to its maturity.

14   **A**   Share capital of any business is the basic and permanent sum subscribed by the shareholders to the business.

15   **A**   Assets and liabilities need to be balanced both in terms of their size and when they are due.

Chapter 7 – International Loan and Bond Markets

1	**A**	They do not necessarily have to involve lending to governments, although they often do.
2	**B**	Given the size of the sums usually involved, they tend to be faster to arrange because the risk is spread across a range of banks, each of which does not have to spend a long while assessing a huge loan, rather it can take a view on its small portion of the overall loan as being less risky than one large sum.
3	**B**	A bank involved in a syndicate is able to lend a lesser amount than if it had to lend the whole sum of the loan and thus can spread its risk.
4	**A**	To take overall charge, assess the initial request for a loan and to act responsibly towards all the parties with regard to all aspects of the enterprise.
5	**B**	The bulk of funding comes from the participating banks, but there is no hard and fast rule.
6	**C**	Cancellation of the loan is usually allowed.
7	**A**	Syndicated loans are usually unsecured. They are also made to organisations that have access to first class legal advice so to protect their investments from the risks in such a situation. The banks tend to have contracts biased in their favour.
8	**D**	It is there as a back-up in the very unlikely event of the London market not being available.
9	**B**	The answer says it all.
10	**C**	Investment banks find purchasers.
11	**A**	It is simply the return to the purchaser when measured as a percentage.
12	**C**	The huge supply of institutional funds has meant that the market has been able to issue larger bond issues.
13	**A**	One is a traded bond that can be realised at any time for a market price, the other is a loan which the investor must hold until maturity.
14	**B**	The underwriter(s) guarantee, for a fee, that if the bond issue is not fully subscribed, then they will buy up the remaining balance.
15	**D**	These are the three main risk factors that anyone who buys bonds needs to take into account when deciding to buy or not.

Chapter 8 – International Banking Risk

1   **D**   It is complex subject but in essence, the risk arises because one country's law is not usually enforceable in another so it is quite possible that contracts might not be possible to enforce with all the resultant risks.

2   **A**   Although this is one example, it is a US case and therefore only persuasive in the UK and possibly not of any value in other countries.

3   **B**   It is an international agreement which promises that the parties will enforce contract debts when they are cross border.

4   **A**   The case *(Libyan Arab Bank Foreign Bank v Bankers Trust 1987)* ruled that only UK law can apply in the UK. It also specified that in this instance as the case was brought in England, it was English law which applied. Presumably if brought in Scotland, Scottish law would apply although this is not specifically clear.

5   **A**   Provided the legal authorities abide by their agreement, it makes eurocurrency deposits easier to obtain repayment for as domestic currency.

6   **D**   Any bond is simply a promise to pay a sum of money when or if something happens. The when or if could be the passage of time, an act of default, failure to perform, confirmation of goodwill in relation to a tender, return of an advance payment and so on. But underneath it all, it is a promise to pay if (or when) something happens.

7   **D**   This is not too difficult to do, so long as loans and deposits are carefully watched on a day to day and hour by hour basis.

8   **D**   All of the above points and more might mean that a country is more or less risky to deal with than another.

9   **A**   The surplus must be in foreign currency so at first sight, it suggests that the country is able to finance its foreign debt from this.

10   **D**   Its overseas borrowings are 1.5 times its annual exports.

11   **A**   It is a measure of the back-up that a country has to pay for its imports, should its export income or domestic wealth fail for some reason. It is therefore a measure to some degree of the reliability of the country to pay its debts, and of course, loans.

12   **D**   There is always a danger of dealing with any non-democratic country or dictatorship. People do not like being bossed around and may rebel. Rebellions can lead to new governments which can change the economic outlook significantly.

13   **D**   Any or all of these methods would spread risk across countries; whether they all, or some of them would work can only be assessed once the deals are complete and monies repaid.

14   **A**   It restructured its debt which is the same thing as defaulting.

15   **A**   It is better to take a pragmatic view and show a realistic figure for what the debts are worth in the balance sheet, rather than some fictional figure which shows what they were once worth.

Chapter 9 – Securitisation and Globalisation

1   **A**   The issue of bonds or notes which are negotiable and therefore saleable as a means of raising finance.

2   **C**   Intermediation is what the banks do when they bring customers with excess funds into contact with those who do not have enough, i.e. they act as an intermediary.

3   **D**   The alternatives all contribute to the general position that bond borrowing is cheaper than bank borrowing for organisations with reasonable credit ratings.

4   **B**   Excess private and institutional wealth particularly in Japan and Germany was tapped via the bond market to fund the debt. The number of US sovereign bonds in circulation grew as a result and the securitised market grew accordingly.

5   **D**   The banks bought and sold all types of bonds, in addition to issuing them to obtain cash.

6   **A**   The banks underwrote the issues for a fee and made money that way, sometimes selling the bonds eventually for a profit, sometimes holding them for the income.

7   **D**   All of the above factors combined to encourage the rise of bond dealing and securitisation.

8   **B**   The bank still enjoys income (in effect) from the mortgages as it has exchanged them for cash. But the cash will appear on the balance sheet whereas any liability that the bank may have had for any of the mortgages that go bad will be carried by the SPV bondholders.

9   **A**   It still receives the interest payments and then passes on to the SPV any funds needed to cover the bondholders' coupon. It is in its interest to keep the latter as low as possible so that it can keep as much of the former as possible.

10   **A**   At one time, banks held vast amounts of information which they held carefully but which allowed them to make lending decisions without sharing this with outsiders. The introduction of cheap IT has enabled bond investors to undertake the same type of assessments of potential borrowers as banks do for their customer and over which they once held a monopoly. Consequently, the bond market is much more open to all.

11   **B**   You can call in a loan at face value and stand a good chance of getting it back, particularly if it is secured. You can wait for a loan to mature and you probably will get it all back, plus interest. But with a bond, you pay your money up front and the price can change with the markets, regardless sometimes of the underlying value of the issuer. Thus your 'loan' can be wiped out in terms of value overnight and your bank's balance sheet could be stripped of its assets as a result.

12   **C**   It could be argued that all are valid and they probably are. But what set the others off was the losses that banks incurred as a result of buying vast numbers of securitised debts and the value then falling, which resulted in other banks refusing to lend to them due to the lack of clarity on the size of their asset base and ability to repay, even over night.

13   **D**   It can be secured or not and is usually for less than a year's maturity.

14   **D**   The secondary market for non-USCP is more active than the primary simply because the dates of paper tend to be longer, so more is traded than with USCP.

15 **A** ECP is any commercial paper that is short term and issued in a currency which is any other than that of the country in which it is issued.

Chapter 10 – Economic Monetary Union (EMU)

1   **C**   The effective removal of exchange rates across the member states was a key feature of the EMS.

2   **A**   Speculation on exchange rates caused currencies to be withdrawn or to be expelled from time to time, sterling being one.

3   **D**   The Maastricht Treaty.

4   **D**   All of these are the three main principals of European Fiscal Policy.

5   **C**   These rather familiar problems were the downfall of the Union.

6   **C**   It was a scheme to enable less strong states to enter the euro which did not meet the original convergence and entry requirements. Some might say as such, that D was an equally valid answer!

7   **D**   Greece.

8   **A**   It only eliminated exchange rate and risk between the user countries. The risk remains elsewhere for euro users and other countries.

9   **B**   The ECB set rates for the stronger countries not the weaker ones, in the main Germany and France. The rates were low and applied to all members. Cheap money led to a building boom and that set off price inflation.

10   **D**   Not one single benefit that was expected to accrue to the public finances generally has been seen, other than in the strongest of the euro countries.

11   **D**   The expected rise of the euro by some as a reserve currency has not happened for all of these reasons and more. It simply does not have the confidence of the world to rise to this status.

12   **B**   It means that the government cannot manage interest rates via the central bank (or in the case of the UK, the Central Bank directly) therefore it is at the mercy of whatever authority sets the rates and whatever agenda it is required to follow, hence the root of the problems of the so called PIGS countries in the EU.

13   **C**   The states which make up the EU comprise the longest surviving and largest free trade area in the world.

14   **D**   Not all ten are waiting to join the euro (the UK is one of the ten) but some of them aspire to join.

15   **C**   France and Germany exceeded the prescribed budget deficit of 3% and stood to be fined under the pact. The pact was therefore suspended as they refuse to be fined, despite smaller countries such as The Netherlands and Austria having complied with the pact with some difficulties in the past.

Chapter 11 – Public Finance

1   **C**   The two main reasons why public finance is raised is to provide for government spending needs and more recently, to re-distribute wealth.

2   **B**   Taxes are payments from organisations and individuals to the state which are compulsory either by virtue of residence or existence, or because the payer has done something (e.g. bought a taxable item).

3   **A**   If demand is constant, then the income from a tax on a product or service can easily be increased by increasing the rate charged.

4   **C**   A tax is progressive when those who earn relatively more than those who earn relatively less pay a higher proportion of their income in taxation.

5   **D**   The tipping point is where, if more tax is charged, the national income will start to reduce and thus reduce taxation income.

6   **A**   The UK operates a progressive system.

7   **B**   Marginal taxation is the sum charged to each portion of taxable income. Average is the rate that applies to a payer's income when all the marginal rates have been applied.

8   **A**   The main place of residence of the taxpayer is not subject to CGT.

9   **B**   A regressive tax is not one which is charged on income, so it tends to hit poorer people more than richer ones, relatively speaking.

10   **C**   Smuggling provides goods to a market on which no taxation is charged. It therefore removes the taxation income from the state and creates a loss to the government when otherwise, people would have bought taxed goods and the government would have received the requisite income.

11   **A**   A move to indirect taxation will inevitably increase prices as the additional tax levied will form part of the price of goods and services.

12   **C**   Although car manufacturing has in the past been supported and owned by the government, current thinking is that this and other commercial activities are much best left to the private sector.

13   **B**   Merit goods and services are those which address personal needs, but which are provided for certain categories of subjects by the government, free or at reduced cost.

14   **B**   The same amount of money is available in the economy but it is in different places. Therefore although the overall amount of demand will probably not change, it will change the pattern of demand.

15   **C**   It is what happens when an economy cannot repay the debt that it is carrying even when it is operating at its usual levels of activity.

Chapter 12 – Financial Crisis 2007 – 2009

1   **D**   All of these contributed to the crisis and together caused it.

2   **C**   Originators who were going to sell lending on had little or no encouragement to undertake due care when assessing loan prospects so they tended to lend recklessly.

3   **B**   All of the above combined to fuel the crisis.

4   **B**   They were bought by and sold on by a huge range of banks worldwide and soon spread the risk that any default carried.

5   **C**   A bubble is almost the reverse of a panic and when one bursts, a panic is created with people trying to get out of whatever investment it is that the bubble represents. Thus it is increasingly difficult and quickly impossible to sell the asset even at a loss. Therefore risks cannot be diversified.

6   **C**   LIBOR is set to accommodate a premium to cover the risk of one bank lending to another in case of default by the borrower. When the lenders do not know which banks hold toxic assets, they become very reluctant to lend, or they refuse to lend, to each other. To reflect this, the rate of interest, LIBOR, rose very markedly in 2006.

7   **C**   It is what it says, a last resort for liquidity and if news leaks out, then there will be a serious danger that customers will lose confidence in the bank needing the facilities and cause a run on the bank.

8   **D**   The takeover for virtually no money suggested that this huge international player was more or less insolvent and that it was hard to sell it, or even to give it away.

9   **A**   It relied too much on wholesale short term funding for long term loans, something that a bank's customers are told never to do.

10 **D**   The banks had little liquidity and needed what they had to shore up their own position, let alone that of their borrowing customers. They dare not take risks by lending it and risking their own situations.

11 **A**   They did this to encourage companies and individuals to spend more.

12 **C**   The banks needed cash and HM Government took new ordinary and preference shares as a means of securing its massive cash injections.

13 **D**   The purchase of assets, usually government debt, so as to pump new money into the banking system.

14 **D**   All these things contributed to the 'herd instinct' and a general wish not to recognise what was happening.

15 **D**   Political and economic history is full of information which ought to have showed up the likelihood of the crisis and it always does, for every crisis. But when people have lots of money and easy credit, the hard stories that history sometimes has to tell lack fashion and the people telling them are not popular. It will happen again.

Chapter 13 – Bank Regulation

1   **A**   There is no requirement as such for management to hold professional qualifications in banking.

2   **D**   All of the reasons given in both A and C are why banks are regulated. In addition, they hold most of the financial fire power of a country. Governments need to have some control over this and they do it using regulation.

3   **C**   Banks are usually highly geared and rely on relatively short term deposits that might or might not be renewed when the term is up, or which are repayable on demand.

4   **A**   Any losses have to be carried by the bank's capital which will reduce as a result, although this might not be evident immediately in the balance sheet as losses and profits are constantly being made.

5   **C**   The provision of a stable banking system and to try to limit damages to bank depositors is the main combined aim of prudential regulation and control.

6   **C**   Both the banks and their customers have in the past placed too much reliance on the regulator's prudential controls rather than applying skill and professional judgement in the case of the banks and reasonable care and common sense in the case of customers.

7   **A**   Banks have in the past worked on the basis that they are so important to the economy, even if they fail the government will bail them out and this has happened. It encourages wreckless risk taking as a result.

8   **B**   The regulator sets a minimum ratio for liquidity and defines what assets can be counted into that ratio.

9   **C**   They provide a minimum ratio of capital to assets to act as a buffer for any bad debts that have to be written off.

10 **D**   All are uses of capital in a bank.

11 **A**   It created a much more equal situation for banks in the developed world to compete, regardless of their capital position.

12 **A**   It will have to provide more capital. Where this comes from is up to the bank, but selling more shares would dilute the current shareholders' holdings so is not likely to be a popular option given a constant level of business. More likely is the putting to capital of any profit, rather than distributing it as dividend.

13 **C**   The banking regulator of each country sets the individual rates for each bank in their country, but the minimum ratio is 8% under the Basle II Accord.

14 **A**   Loans that deliver the most profit tend to tie up cash for the longest periods, or are the least easy to sell on the market. Hence, the more profitable loans tend to mitigate against liquidity.

15 **B**   The banks need to be stopped from using retail customers' money to fund high risk investment bank activities.

Chapter 14 – Banking/Financial Environment

1   **D**   All the options have driven the banks to think again.

2   **B**   It is a geometric progression. The more people have to save and/or spend, the more they require basic banking services. As they become wealthier, they need better and wider services beyond those offered by basic banking. Hence the system grows to accommodate such needs.

3   **C**   Deregulation occurred to address a political philosophy which said that competition was good and that it was inhibited by regulation. Hence, the banks went into all manner of other financial activities whilst other providers in those fields went into banking.

4   **A**   Customers accepted cost to a point, but when they saw the same services being provided at ever competitive prices, they lost loyalty and moved to obtain perceived value for money.

5   **A**   Intense competition which resulted in reduced interest rates for riskier loans not providing adequate margins when defaults occurred.

6   **D**   All these factors combined to put the banks into a position where nothing was ever static and they had to change all the time.

7   **B**   There was a move towards high margin personal lending of all types which usually meant more lending than they ought to have done to individuals (high loan to value property lending) and/or charging for anything that they could find to charge for, whereas once it was 'free'. There was also a huge rise in the selling of more or less any 'financial service' that they could persuade customers to accept.

8   **D**   To some extent, all are true. There were few people left to do the still considerable amount of human work that was needed, despite longer term cost savings, vast sums had to be paid to those leaving on redundancy or early retirement packages and for those who remained, large amounts had to be spent on training, re-training and to get them to perform to a required standard, bonus payments.

9   **D**   All these reasons were compelling ones as to why mergers were so attractive.

10   **D**   The banks have retreated from the High Street and dehumanised their services. As a result customers lost contact and a sense of control and trust, which resulted in little, if any, loyalty.

11   **D**   Each of these factors will become increasingly noticeable as the recommendations of the Vickers Report come into play.

12   **C**   Over 70% of people in the UK live in an owner-occupied house. This means that there is a decreasing opportunity for the banks to sell mortgages to those who remain as aspirant owners.

13   **A**   They took too many high risks to boost earnings and often failed as a result.

14   **B**   They exist primarily to serve the customers who own them and their local communities.

15   **C**   Private banking is difficult to precisely to define, but common across all of the private banks is the provision of retail and specialist financial services to high net worth customers.

Chapter 15 – Innovation and Technology in Banking

1   **A**   An expert system is computer based and should replace the skills of a number of human experts.

2   **C**   Automation was introduced to save money by cutting down on expensive staff to do routine transactions. The absence of people though has made banking increasingly seem an impersonal activity for an increasing number of customers.

3   **D**   ATMs can pay a customer's bills.

An ATM is not able to perform any task that requires the creation or termination of a contract.

4   **A**   Telephones and PC banking can do much the same things for the customer. The big difference though is that PCs provide the ability for the customer to see what is happening or what has happened, e.g. the viewing of an account.

5   **C**   Without the cost of a branch network and people to staff it, their costs tend to be significantly lower and they can afford to charge less and pay more.

6   **D**   All of these alternatives are reasons for recording telephone calls.

7   **A**   Computer telephony integration is the linking of these two technologies so that they work in harmony. When one is used the other reacts accordingly to assist the operator in the call centre.

8   **D**   A traditional bank that also uses modern IT delivery methods.

9   **D**   All these factors mitigate against the use of IT based delivery channels to some potential users.

10   **A**   The overwhelming reason which encompasses all the others is that provision of banking over the internet is much cheaper than any other form of banking delivery.

11   **C**   The bank's APP is downloaded to a mobile telephone and then delivery can commence after some identification formalities.

12   **A**   Some smart phones have a swipe facility which allows money to be paid from a bank account to the person or company who has swiped the phone.

13   **C**   It may have levelled off, or may level off, but fewer people visit branches as technology permits easier and simpler access by other means. This means that there is less need for them so fewer opportunities to use them by both customers and the banks for marketing.

14   **D**   There are lots of arguments in favour of retaining branches, but all of these are good ones.

15   **A**   Any computer system is objective since this is the nature of the beast, so when subjective judgement is required, human involvement is essential.

PRACTICE EXAMINATION 1

Question 1

Required

The national income is derived from two main sources.

Consider what these are and explain how they operate to create the National Income. **(30 marks)**

(TOTAL 30 MARKS)

Question 2

Required

(a) It is often said that a country's ability to set its own interest rates is one of the most powerful weapons in its monetary policy arsenal. Explain why this is so? **(6 marks)**

(b) Examine the use of OMOs and contrast their function with that of the manipulation of interest rates. **(9 marks)**

(TOTAL 15 MARKS)

Question 3

Required

(a) Examine the position of London as the major financial centre of the World and explain why it holds this pre-eminent position. **(8 marks)**

(b) Examine and critically appraise the benefits to the UK of having London as the world's chief financial centre. **(12 marks)**

(TOTAL 20 MARKS)

Question 4

Required

(a) Categorise and briefly explain in each case, the main risks which exist in relation to International Banking. **(6 marks)**

(b) Consider the position if a country were to default on its debts, what options are available to the banks which hold that debt and what alternatives are available to deal with the situation.

(6 marks)

(c) Heuirsitics and inferential processes are used in what context and to what purposes in the application of innovative technological systems in banking? **(8 marks)**

(TOTAL 20 MARKS)

Question 5

Required

(a) Examine and discuss the factors that combined to create the banking crisis of 2007-9. Your answer should place particular emphasis on both the strategic issues and technical capabilities of the banks' operations. **(10 marks)**

(b) Why is it that it is unwise for banks to place too much reliance on the use of wholesale rather than depositors' funds? **(5 marks)**

(TOTAL 15 MARKS)

Answer 1

The national income comes from two sources, these are:

- People or organisations working for other people or organisations for which they receive payment (i.e. income, usually wages).

- People or organisations owning or having what are known as the factors of production. These factors of production are land, labour, capital and enterprise. When the owners of these physical assets or those with entrepreneurial spirit use it, then they are rewarded by payment from those who need access to these factors, either by means of rent, payment for services rendered, interest and the like.

Because everyone renders different services or provides different things, then it is almost inevitable that each person's income will be different from that of another, whilst the same applies to organisations. This results in inequality of income across the population as most people obtain their income by in effect, renting their time and skills to an employer who in return pays them a wage or salary for this. Of course, many people have additional income as a result of investing spare money in various ways, the most obvious being in a bank account, from which they derive income. In any such case, they own some of one of the factors of production, in this case capital. Their wage income is supplemented by the income that they obtain from the bank for the use of their capital. Thus they own, albeit perhaps fractionally, some of one of the factors of production.

If the government is for whatever reason, seeking to make incomes more equal, they can tax those with what they regard as too much income and redistribute it to those with what they regard as too little and they do this all the time in the UK. This though is merely a re-distribution of income, not a new part of the national income. The only thing which contribute to an increase in the National Income is 'new money' earned either for the performance of services or for the contribution made by ownership of one or more of the factors of production. The total income depends entirely on the sum of these two figures which is the same as the total volume of production of goods and services.

It also follows that one person's expenditure is another person's income; the more that is spent, the more the National Income increases. If this concept is carried to its logical conclusion, we can see that not only is the National Income the same as the total volume of production of goods and services, but it also has to be the same as the total expenditure. Thus, Production = Income = Expenditure.

If an economy has something that can measure these three figures, then it is able to say how much is the national income. As money is used in all modern economies, the national income is quoted in terms of money.

The income comes from:

- Wages and salaries (in return for labour)
- Interest (on capital)
- Rent (for land and buildings and anything else that is inanimate and hired)
- Profit (in return for enterprise)

Expenditure comes from:

- Consumption of goods and services
- Investment of spare money

Production (i.e. output) creates the goods and services that results in expenditure which results in income of the above various types.

The flow of income inwards and expenditure outwards does not really matter in terms of whether it is by individuals or organisations so long as the flow happens and people and organisations are both in receipt and spend. Because overall, the flows will be equal to each other, any increase in the flow coming from exports (hence additional income beyond the domestic balance) and increase in the speed of flow domestically, which will result in additional profit, which results in additional expenditure which, in turn, results in additional income.

(30 marks)

Answer 2

(a) The reason is that the base rate is the minimum interest rate that a central bank will lend to a bank when lender of last resort facilities are sought. If lending is more or less expensive, people and organisations will be discouraged or encouraged to borrow. Money is borrowed so that it can be spent and when it is spent, it contributes to the national income. Thus, the national income is to a significant extent tied to the availability of credit. Governments by changing the interest rate charged by the central bank to banks generally can thus effect the demand for money in an economy, the availability of credit and the size of the national income. It is obvious therefore that this ability has to be one of the main means by which a government can influence spending and consumption and therefore income. **(6 marks)**

(b) OMOs or open market operations are another method by which the Bank of England influences the economy. In this case, unlike the direct setting of base rate for its lending to other banks, the Bank buys and sells gilts that are already on the market in the same way, but on a much bigger scale, than any investor might do. The reason though is different. Where an ordinary investor buys for income or in anticipation of a turn on the price the Bank trades in them so as to influence their price and to influence commercial interest rates charged by the market. By selling them, the overall price of gilts goes down as the market has more available, by buying them, the overall price goes up as the stock available to purchase is reduced.

If the bank wishes to prevent interest rates from rising, it could simply adjust the base rate to the other banks. This is though a very public way of acting and can send out all sorts of messages that might not be beneficial in terms of the prospects for the economy. It can also lack subtlety in that it is done as a semi-permanent measure that effects all the banks. By buying gilts, the bank pumps additional money into the economy (usually by buying them from the banks or in any event, the vendors will put the money into the banks) and thus, there is more to lend and interest rates will either go down (because there is more money to 'sell' so it will be 'cheaper', just like any market place) or at least remain the same. The opposite applies when gilts are bought.

In addition, the bank uses OMOs to send out messages that it expects its base rate to rise or fall, by its actions. It will be obvious that for OMOs to work there must be a mature, deep and liquid market for gilts. **(9 marks)**

Answer 3

(a) London remains the pre-eminent financial centre of the world. It has the largest concentration of foreign banks anywhere in the world and about 20% of the world's lending, one way or another, passes through or is done in London. The reasons for this are partly practical and partly historical, but remain very valid today, otherwise the various financial institutions, particularly the banks, would go elsewhere, to find what they consider to be the best place to do business. That so few, if any have actually done this, despite posturing and threats, demonstrates the hold that London has over the global industry.

Primarily, this is because London is in the UK which has a very stable political and social structure. The UK government although it does interfere as do all governments; it does so much less than many, indeed most other jurisdictions.

Sterling's pre-war role as the main reserve currency of the world and the UK's role as the largest imperial power ever gave London an unparalleled expertise in the conduct of overseas business relating to trade and investment. This is supported by a stable domestic banking system (hence one of the Government's reasons for saving it in 2008) and superb telecommunications and other necessary infrastructure.

The Bank of England provides the very minimum of regulation upon foreign banks' non-sterling deposit and loan business, they are more or less left to get on with it. This has encouraged the establishment of large numbers of overseas banks in London, where they can be free from sometimes oppressive regulation from their own or other jurisdictions.

London is also fortunate in that geographically, it sits across time zones that enable business to be done there between the Far East and the USA in one trading day and of course, the international language, English, the mother tongue.

A looming threat to London's position comes in the form of the 2017 EU referendum. Should the UK leave the EU, it could have disastrous effects for financial services in London.   **(8 marks)**

(b)   The benefits come at several levels. First of all, the local banking systems of London provide essential money transfer and other retail banking services to the various City firms and institutions, just as they do to other businesses in London. This means that they in turn become experts in the needs of those involved with the Stock Market, Insurance, Shipping, Commodities, Futures and the like. Thus, it is possible to create complete deals in London without the need to go to other centres of expertise. This in itself creates huge financial benefits to the UK, it creates wealth in itself and encourages more growth in terms of international business being done in London.

The services provided by the banks are of course available to British businesses in addition to those of overseas banks. This means that domestic business has exceptional access, the like of which does not exist overseas, to the expertise and contacts of the banks in the City.

The presence of all the banks and their expertise has resulted in new and innovative lending methods being provided and made available to British Industry. The overseas banks in the UK are usually not here just to access the facilities of the City, but are also keen to do domestic business, hence they add a new element of competition to the services that corporates are looking for and ensure that the domestic market in which they become involved is even more competitively priced.

All these activities pay tax to central and local government, create both direct and indirect employment which of course all contributes considerably to the national income and balance of payments via what are usually termed 'invisible earnings'.

The fact that London is such an important place in the global finance industry also creates employment in legal and accountancy services, IT, printing, building, telecommunications and a whole range of other activities, even restaurants, coffee shops and high quality consumer goods, as the money filters down through the system.

The City is responsible for about 140,000 jobs and 3% of the UK's GDP. Invisible earnings in monetary terms are worth about £20bn per year to the balance of payments.   **(12 marks)**

Answer 4

(a)   The main factors are as follows:

- **Eurocurrency deposit risk**. The risk that a bank which is holding the international deposit will fail. This can be mitigated against by a range of measures, including having the bank involved as a wholly owned subsidiary rather than a part of the overseas bank, so that it benefits from whatever local government deposit guarantees there are to protect depositors.

- **Banks and bonds**. The risk that a customer of a bank will not perform to contract, in which case a bank is able to provide for a fee a guarantee that there will be no financial loss to the purchaser (usually the customer of the UK bank's customer).

- **Foreign currency exposure**. The risk that exchange rates might adversely shift, which can be mitigated against by hedging.

- **Country risk**. The danger that one of or both the countries involved may become politically unstable which can be mitigated against by research into the country, insurance against revolution and the like and/or diversification of business across a range of countries to reduce the risk.   **(6 marks)**

(b)   It is always possible that in an extreme situation, a country could simply repudiate its debt and literally refuse to pay. Without an army to march in (as the UK did with Egypt in the 1880s) there is little that the banks can do to enforce the obligation.

Some form of restructuring could take place, where the debtor nation agrees to repay the loans over a longer period. Here, the banks effectively repay themselves with new loans to the defaulting country, which is what happened over the winter of 2011/12 when Greece, to all intents and purposes defaulted, although the EU did not like to refer to it as such at the time.

Another method might be that the banks agree to write off a portion of the debt. Again, this happened with Greece and with Argentina in 2001 when the latter was only able to pay 30 cents on each US dollar owed.

The last method to try to pull something from such a disaster (unless someone invents something new in the future) is for the lending banks to convert their debt into an equity stake in the country, by a stake or bonds. Here, the amount owed in, say sterling, is converted into the local currency and then the stake is converted in turn into shares or bonds in local industry. The banks might get a return from this by way of increased share or bond prices or a dividend or coupon payment (which given the position nationally seems a bit unlikely, but the chance is there and the banks do hold assets, rather than totally worthless government paper). They could also convert their loans into government securities if they are not already so secured, but these are bound to trade at a considerable discount, so in effect it is the same as writing off a portion of the debt.

(6 marks)

(c)   These terms refer to IT based judgemental and reasoning systems that are built into a so-called expert system of the type that are used by banks to both supplement and replace knowledge.

Their use enables IT systems to apply a degree of subjectivity to decisions when this is required, such as in making a lending assessment from pure knowledge that is fed into the system. Knowledge is entered into the system in a specific format which the so-called shell of the programme is able to digest. This then interfaces with the heuristic and inferential elements to arrive at a conclusion which ought to take account of the subjective issues involved.

A subjective assessment sometimes requires the application of experience and a gut-feel which usually, if it is be of any value, uses such human traits as intuition and experience as well occasionally a gut feeling and intelligent guesswork, which is it very difficult for any IT system to replicate. Hence, it is unlikely that for the sort of decisions that require such human characteristics (which are very expensive to use at all levels of such decision making) any other than a more or less objective decision will be arrived at. However, for higher level decisions when human intervention is essential if risk is to be considered from every angle, such systems can be used to a point, where information is produce and recommendations made, but the final analysis will almost invariably come from a person.

(8 marks)

Answer 5

(a) There were many factors but one huge driver was the US housing market. This is usually seen as the prime mover. There was a steady rise in prices to July 2006 but the market was showing all the classic signs of a financial bubble which could not go on. This was fed by the US banks which were lending more and more whilst applying weaker and weaker lending criteria to lower and lower creditworthy customers.

It would be fair to say that the industry drove a dilution of professional standards in a never ending quest for increased profits, regardless of how reckless this was. In an extension of this, incredibly, much of the resultant debt was packed into specially created companies (special purpose vehicles) which were sold on to other countries on the basis that the loans in them were granted by highly reputable banks (such as Lehman Brothers and Bear Stearns) with AAA credit ratings. This allowed some financial institutions in effect to enter the US mortgage lending market, which they did with abandon and apparently without much thought that things might go wrong. Consequently when they did, the so called 'toxic debt' was spread all over the world and to this day, we are not entirely sure where it all is, or what is or what is not likely ultimately to become toxic.

This process was stoked by a general liberalisation of the regulation applied to banks all over the world, although there were notable exceptions such as in Australia and Canada. At the same time, inflation control (chiefly monetary) policies looked at monetary price inflation but ignored the huge increases in asset prices (such as houses) whilst all of this was certainly not helped by several important regulators in a range of countries (including the UK) simply not doing their job properly. The banks were allowed to use the wholesale markets to raise funds which were readily available and allowed fast growth, instead of the traditional proven methods of growing slowly using depositors' funds to lend on in a prudent manner.

Modern technology and what come might at the time have been termed innovation (which others have called dangerous and ill-informed practices) also had a considerable part to play in permitting the management of the banks to implement these strategies. The ability of the US banks to securitise debt could not have happened without their ability to sell the special purpose vehicles containing what turned out to be huge amount of toxic debt; this was only permitted by the banks using IT facilities which marketed and transferred such items around the world in a matter of seconds.

It is important to see such IT capacity not as a benign force which sits awaiting innocent use; like the technologies that permit nations to use arms for good or bad purposes, in the wrong hands, IT can be used to support the most alarming of management strategies and enable the strangest of ideas to happen. A example of this was with Northern Rock which was a major contributor to the UK banking crisis of 2008-9. Here, the unqualified Chief Executive decided to concentrate on using funds from the London wholesale market rather than the traditional method of obtaining funds from depositors, which would speed up the availability of funds for his bank to lend.

This could not have been done without the facility, provided by sophisticated IT, to access the London money market on a more or less constant basis, to feed the ever faster need of Northern Rock to buy new funds and, more importantly as it turned out to renew existing borrowings. This practice, benign in itself turned out to be the ruin of a once great organisations and demonstrates how, in the wrong hands, IT, usually seen as a force for good, for cost cutting and making things easier, actually enabled the whole operation to more or less literally implode, whilst in itself, the system did nothing wrong. It was the banking equivalent of the ammunition store exploding.

Finally, matters were not helped by a few of the banks (at least in the UK) having got rid of experienced staff who were academically qualified and replacing them with a sales force of people who did not know how to lend, simply how to feed information into a computer. Few of the chief executives, chairmen or board members of the banks held any banking qualifications. **(10 marks)**

(b)   If reliance is placed on wholesale funds, the bank is lending long term to customers and borrowing short term from the markets. This means that there will be a more or less constant shortage of funds by a bank in such a position, as the wholesale market lends only for months, rather than years. Depositors' funds cannot of course be relied upon forever, but they are more likely to remain than the certain need to renew short term wholesale borrowings. If a bank does this, then it is wholly or very dependent upon the (mostly) London market which, if for some reason ceases to be able to provide credit (as happened in 2008) will find that it simply runs out cash. This is exactly what happened to Northern Rock and its unqualified management, the result being a crash in confidence in the organisation and a run on its branches.   **(5 marks)**

PRACTICE EXAMINATION 2

Question 1

Required

Examine the proposition 'The pursuit of profits conflicts with the need for liquidity' and demonstrate how banks are able (or not) to reconcile the two conflicting demands.

Your answer should seek to identify the strategic demands placed upon banks to produce profits whilst retaining adequate liquidity and also the challenges which this creates in the operational management of such a need. **(30 marks)**

(TOTAL 30 MARKS)

Question 2

Required

(a) Examine the reasons why NS&I have significant advantages over retail banks? **(5 marks)**

(b) Distinguish the differences between a mutual bank/building society and the commercial retail banks. **(5 marks)**

(c) Hypothesise reasons why there are estimated to be about three million unbanked socially excluded people in the UK. **(5 marks)**

(TOTAL 15 MARKS)

Question 3

Required

(a) Describe what is meant by inflation. **(8 marks)**

(b) Examine the ways by which inflation can be controlled. **(12 marks)**

(TOTAL 20 MARKS)

Question 4

Required

(a) Differentiate briefly between the different types of financial markets that exist. **(6 marks)**

(b) Distinguish between a eurocurrency and a eurodollar. **(6 marks)**

(c) Your Study Text suggests that a recent development in banking delivery has been the introduction of telephone banking. Discuss how this works and what recent innovative changes have happened to make it even more attractive to banks as a delivery channel. **(8 marks)**

(TOTAL 20 MARKS)

Question 5

Required

(a) Reflect critically about the start of the euro and demonstrate why some commentators consider that it is turning out to be a disaster. **(10 marks)**

(b) Discuss why the loss of exchange rate flexibility for those countries joining the euro was such a problem. **(5 marks)**

(TOTAL 15 MARKS)

Answer 1

Banks need cash and book-entry money, electronic money, available on demand which is known as liquidity, to be able to repay their customers who may demand repayment of their deposits at no notice. If they do not have such access then they may have to decline requests for repayment of balances from customers. If this happens then customers will lose confidence in the bank and there is a good chance that there will be a 'run' on it, as happened with Northern Rock some years ago.

However, the more money that banks retain as liquidity the less they are able to lend to borrowing customers as the funds retained as their 'liquidity cushion' are simply sitting awaiting use in case of need. This means that they are not making profit on the potential additional lending that the funds could be used to create; it is thus very tempting for banks to find a means by which they can use as much of their liquidity as possible for lending to make profits, whilst retaining their customers' confidence in their ability to repay balances.

This conflict is heightened by the fact that longer term loans tend to be more profitable (they only need to be arranged once and can attract better rates of interest) than short term ones but of course, they tie up liquidity for a similarly longer period. In any event, the more that banks lend, the more profit they make and the more comes from increased fees and transactional activities. This makes the more recent channels of distribution more attractive to banks than the traditional branch based systems, which latter are very expensive to operate. Hence, for mass market banking, banks find modern electronic based systems much more attractive not only due to the increased gross profits that they produce because of reduced costs, but because some of those profits can be used to support the banks need for liquidity rather than being diverted to being distributed as dividends to shareholders.

Banks though do not retain huge proportions of their liabilities to customers in liquid funds, otherwise they would in effect be sitting on a large pile of cash which was doing nothing other than providing comfort in case a large proportion of their deposits were to be withdrawn. In practice, so long as customers retain their confidence in the bank, few will demand more than a tiny proportion of their deposits back at any one time. Banks have so many customers and there is so much transactional activity that even if one customer were to withdraw all their funds, others will not and others may be depositing, to make up what has been withdrawn. As a general rule, about 8% of the on-call deposits needs to be retained to meet on-call demands, although about 70% of bank deposits are theoretically repayable on demand.

There is an obvious need for profit, but it is perhaps heightened in banks where figures are watched by the industry and analysts in close detail and comparisons between banks are constant. There is little room for sentiment in banking and predatory takeovers are not uncommon. These often happen when one bank is seen to be less profitable than another, when the second can move to takeover the first with the prospect of increased profits being dangled before the shareholders of the less profitable organisation.

Such takeovers usually result in the boards and management of the organisation that has been taken over losing their jobs, so there can be intense pressure on these groups of people to lend as much as possible at as high a rate as possible to keep profitability as high as possible.

It therefore follows that for a bank to continue to trade, there is constant conflict between the need for liquidity and the need to use as much as possible of its spare funds to lend. Banks therefore will seek out the most profitable ways of doing business, primarily to retain their liquidity but also to enable them to pay dividends, increase shareholder value and to fend off hostile takeovers. A bank will retain a certain amount, at least that required by the regulator, in the case of some more prudent banks rather more than this, in cash or assets that can be converted to cash at virtually no notice, such as British government securities. With such assets, it is important of course that the conversion process does not result in a loss; otherwise this in itself amounts to a contraction of liquidity.

A bank's assets (excepting fixed assets such as buildings and equipment) range from physical cash through balances with other banks and at the Bank of England, to loans, commercial paper, longer term investments whilst at the other end of the scale are long term loans such as mortgage loans to private customers and commercial long term loans to business customers. A sudden demand for repayment by customers with at-call funds obviously cannot be met from the assets at the latter end of the spectrum without calling in loans and overdrafts, although theoretically the latter are always subject to repayment on demand by the bank. The assets at the lower end of this spectrum will not really be performing profitably, although sometimes significant sums of cash can be lent out overnight very profitably. Usually though, the further one gets to cash, the less profit is being made from the assets involved and therefore, the more pressure there is on the bank to convert them into other better performing assets.

Thus, although banks may hold significantly large portfolios of assets, what is available to repay customers on demand is a tiny proportion of this sum. In practice, banks only need to meet demand for repayment on a day to day basis from those 'at-sight' customers who request instant repayment (usually not of all their balances and usually a very small proportion of the whole amount deposited by such customers), maturing short notice deposits or those maturing with fixed but longer term dates and their commitments to lend, which of course need to be available in liquid form.

Apart from investment banking activities which are purely speculative lending is usually far more profitable than other forms of investment for banks. Staff at all levels are given targets for lending and commitments are made well in advance for such lending to be available. This though supposes that there will be adequate liquid funds available to meet these commitments, when the borrowing customers come to draw out the advances. Failure to meet these commitments to borrowing customers would have the same effect on confidence in the bank as would its failure to pay out depositors on demand. In addition, there needs to be adequate liquidity in place to cover the agreed overdraft limits of customers, even if they are not at present fully utilised.

Banks have access to the London money market and so to some extent can meet their short term needs for liquidity by relying upon borrowing from that source. But of course, the availability of such funding is only there at a cost which depends upon the credit rating of the bank and as we saw in 2007/8, it can dry up if the market loses confidence generally or in specific organisations. It was over reliance on this form of liquidity that did for Northern Rock.

Thus, there is a constant conflict between a bank's need to have ready funds available to repay its at-call commitments and its need to use such liquid funds for lending, which is far more profitable than simply holding them in case of need. The balancing of these conflicting demands is one of the skills needed of bank management and one which they showed in the recent past that they sadly lacked, indeed in the case of some banks that astonishingly they simply were not aware of. It is the job of individual banks to maintain adequate liquidity and if need be, to accept that this will result in reduced profitability, which is preferable to the organisation being extinguished as a result of not being able to meet its obligations. However, behind prudent domestic management are the regulators who also in the past have not entirely inspired confidence in their ability to recognise this essential conflict that has to be present in all banks. It is to be hoped that when this regulation returns to the Bank of England, the former confidence in the regulators will be restored and people will be able confidently to do business with sound banks run by bankers, rather than salesmen.

At one time it was relatively easy for banks to see what they had as liquid funds but today with much of their liquidity lost to physical visibility in electronic book entry money, banks have to invest in the best possible technology to keep themselves up to date and to ensure that their systems are able to keep track of their positions. One outcome of the banking crisis of 2008/9 was a requirement that banks are able to produce very frequent updates of their positions as regards liquidity and this has placed a need on all banks to have the best possible infrastructure and IT technology. The need for liquidity is a basic of banking but today, it is combined with the need to choose the best possible type of delivery channels to keep costs as low as possible, to provide deposit and lending services that are not only highly attractive but which also cost as little as possible to ensure that profits are high enough to contribute significantly to liquidity.

It therefore follows that the need for profitability and liquidity are closely tied together and although each is to some extent in conflict they are interdependent and one cannot be without the other. This has always been the case although in the past they were much more easily managed in the absence of the technology that is available today. Ironically, the availability of so many methods of delivery and such sophisticated methods of accounting infrastructure all designed to make things easier, simpler and cheaper, can have the opposite effect.

They enable banks to obtain a competitive edge over their rivals, yet require as a result intense management skills to balance the resultant opportunities to make more money and to keep costs down. No longer can we see simply a two way conflict between liquidity and profitability, but rather a multifaceted challenge that still pits these two traditional forces in the game, but combines them with the chances of increased profits due to cost containment opportunities against the massive competition as a result of all banks having access to such facilities and infrastructure. The speed of this change is in real danger of imperilling the essential need for liquidity and profitability and it behoves the banks well to see this and to manage what is now at least a four way dynamic conflict, that grew from the traditional two way one of merely profit v liquidity. **(30 marks)**

Answer 2

(a) The main reason is that deposits at NS & I (National Savings and Investments) are guaranteed completely by the state, whereas the state guarantee applies to only £85,000 of any deposit by an individual in a retail bank in the UK.

NS & I raises funds for the government through a range of savings products that are sold to the public via post offices, some banks and the internet. Interest rates vary but have never been really spectacular although some offers can be very competitive. On the other hand, they are as safe as any investment can be due to the fact that they are with the government. **(5 marks)**

(b) A mutual bank is one which is owned by its customers and run for their benefit, whilst a commercial retail bank is one which is owned by and run for the benefit of its shareholders. It therefore follows that a commercial bank is likely to put the interests of its owners before those of its customers. This means that customers will tend to be seen as sources of profit as much as the people without who the bank could not operate. Conversely, the customers of a mutual can only be seen by the management in both ownership and customer roles, so the actions of management have to be to ensure the well-being of their customers as much as the need to make a profit, as neither are mutually exclusive.

This difference in ownership has a significant impact on the competitive position of the two types of bank.

It is more than likely that with a commercial bank the need to make profit will be the dominant factor and thus customers will never get the best possible deal as profit will always take away some of the income or increase fees that are paid or charged to customers. It follows that to remain competitive with mutual organisations, commercial banks will have to provide competitive rates of interest and charges, whilst mutuals which do not have the profit imperative will be able to accept lower fees and pay higher rates of interest. To compete on this basis, commercial banks will have to have access to funding at lower rates than a mutual (which can be done given their sheer buying power) or they will have to keep their costs lower, to provide the margin of difference that will make up the lost profit due to their need to reduce fees and increase interest.

Competition is also of course open to commercial banks on the sheer range of services that they are able to offer, which might not be possible to the usually smaller mutual organisations. Finally, although businesses can and do bank with mutual (particularly the Co-op), mutual tend to concentrate in the field of personal business, often manifesting themselves as mortgage lenders in the form of building societies. As such, they cannot offer the full range of services that a commercial bank can and are therefore less attractive to the average customer. **(5 marks)**

(c) Most of these people come from socially deprived parts of the country. They live in what amounts to a cash economy and their only need for credit is to provide cash until the next benefit cheque arrives, or if they are on low wages, until the next pay day, to tide them over. Banks insist and research shows that they do not decline the accounts of such people, but rather that they simply do not ask to open accounts. It is a matter of perception.

As a result, rather than using mainstream banking facilities and reasonably priced credit, they use the services of loan companies which are perceived by many to be not much better than 'loan sharks' who charge very high rates of interest for pay day loans and in extremis, those loans provided by door to door lenders whose recovery practices verge upon or are illegal. To address this the government has encouraged the rise of Credit Unions which seem to be having some success and some commercial banks issue debit cards instead of cheque books, which are used whilst the usual type of relationship is built up, pending the granting of credit facilities. There has been some success with this type of business, beneficial to both parties. **(5 marks)**

Answer 3

(a) Inflation is the rising of prices which results in the decline in the value of money. Over the last twenty years or so, the rate of this decline, the rate of inflation, has been as high as 10% p.a. and as low as 2%. The current target set by the Chancellor of the Exchequer is 2%.

Inflation can be caused by two things. The first is an increase in overall demand when there is not enough supply to fulfil this. The result is that prices rise which is the inflationary effect. It can be overcome by increasing production, which will usually require employment to rise to accommodate the need for increased production. If though total spending continues to outstrip the economy's ability to supply, inflation will remain. Usually, prices start to rise before full employment is reached and not all parts of the economy will reach full employment at the same time. Shortages of skilled workers can be met by immigration with the social tensions that this might create, or just as likely, wages will increase as demand for skilled workers rises, which in turn fuels inflation as there is more money chasing the few goods available.

The other cause of inflation is cost-push, which arises due to prices increasing due to a rise in production costs. This is most likely to arise as a result of increased wages, for whatever reason and was the cause of the rampant inflation of the 1970s when the trade unions' demands for ever increasing wages got out of control.

Overall, inflation is caused by excessive supply of money for whatever reason in an economy. It can only happen if there is money there to fuel it and it can only continue if there is demand there to cause prices to rise, or there is enough money to create more demand than goods, which has the same effect. **(8 marks)**

(b) Inflation is a notoriously difficult thing to control. Overall, it depends on the basic cause and often there is disagreement about this which regularly spills over in to the political area and can cause more trouble in turn.

The basic answer is in all cases to reduce the money supply, so that people will not have enough money to spend. In the short term though this can have drastic outcomes, such as resulting in people not being able to afford to buy food and basic necessities. Therefore, a rather more subtle analysis needs to be done to discover the reasons why inflation is happening.

With demand pull inflation, a very likely cause is that the government is spending more than it is receiving in taxes, resulting in the population having more money to spend and resulting in an unfulfilled rise in demand. Prices take off as a result. One way to address this is to raise taxes simply to reduce the amount of money in circulation. This will make the government unpopular particularly where it is seen to be financing the public sector which is perceived always to be profligate. The government could though simply print money to finance the shortfall, but this in itself sets off further inflation.

Probably a better solution is to cut demand. It could do this by increasing taxes on the private sector, which will not be popular, or it could cut down on what it does and reduce public benefits. It should instead of increasing taxes, and seek to reduce or remove the public sector borrowing requirement.

With cost push, this tends to take on a life of its own, as workers see their peers obtaining more and more money, they naturally want increases themselves. If productivity is linked to wage rises, this ought to address the problem of wage rises being inflationary because the increases will be paid for out of the higher production income. Public sector workers, such as many local authority and government employees, cannot be measured in terms of their monetary outputs and they tend at such times to suffer a decline in their incomes as a result. An incomes policy might be a way round the problem, but these are difficult to apply in practice. There is no real answer to this type of inflation without pain and political strife, as was seen in the 1970s. It took some doing but equilibrium was achieved then, but at considerable cost. **(12 marks)**

Answer 4

(a)   The financial markets are usually split into three groups.

- **A domestic financial market**. Here, most transactions are denominated in the domestic currency, e.g. in the UK transactions are done in sterling.

- **A foreign financial market**. Here, the lender and the borrower are in different countries and the transaction involved will be subject to the regulatory controls of the country in which the funds are raised. For example, if a US company raises sterling in the UK, the transactions will be subject to UK regulations.

- **A eurocurrency market**. This has nothing to do as such with Europe or the euro. It is sometimes referred to as an external market. Here national regulations are avoided by not using facilities in the domestic market of the country in whose currency is involved. For example, a loan in US dollars, raised in London for use by a French company would be a transaction in the eurocurrency market and would not be subject to anyone's regulations.

(6 marks)

(b)   A eurocurrency is any currency held as a timed deposit in a bank located outside the country whose currency is being held. For example, an Australian dollar deposit in London would be a eurocurrency, regardless of which bank held it, because it is in London.

A eurodollar is a timed deposit held in any bank outside the USA, denominated in US dollars. The key factor is if the transaction, be it a deposit or even a loan, is done across the books of a bank that is based in the USA in which case it is not a Eurodollar; or one that is not done across the books in the USA, in which case it is. **(6 marks)**

(c)   The Study Text explains that telephone banking has been a major development in recent years. This enables customers to call into a central call centre and make enquiries about their accounts, where they can also pay bills, make transfers and other such activities.

Most banks now provide this innovative service which gives 24-hour a day access to accounts. Customers do not need a new account to use the service, they simply access their existing ones by quoting a personal identity number and a password which ensures that the person calling has the authority to deal or undertake the desired activities and authorise the transactions.

This removes the need for branches to respond to customer enquiries and for staff to concentrate upon duties which have to be branch based and thus to give a better service to customers using specially designed computer software.

Some banks have even been established whose only contact with the customer is over the telephone. The full range of services is provided - cheque books, plastic cards, automated transfers – whilst the need for access to an ATM is covered by the use of reciprocal facilities with other banks. The first example of this was First Direct, owned wholly by HSBC which although it took some time to gain momentum has now attracted a substantial number of customers.

Large retailers, such as Tescos, are also entering this field. They are able to offer good interest rates as they have no branch costs, and to provide a number of innovative services which combine a number of features that merge several traditional account types.

The growth of this type of banking and call centres has resulted in the harnessing of the technologies of the computer and telephone at the same time by the banking provider. This is known as computer telephone integration. This enables computers and telephones to be linked to help improve the effectiveness of the call centre. The customer's details are shown a screen when they call and this enables the operator to provide an enhanced level of service through the combination of the processing power of computers with the accessibility and convenience of the telephone. It can also be used for outbound calls which saves the advisor time in having to input the customer's details when they are being called. **(8 marks)**

Answer 5

(a)   The European Monetary Union project, the euro, was primarily a political project rather than an economic one, although it had definite economic elements to it. Underlying the whole thing was a wish to tie together, irrevocably, the countries of Europe so that they could never again go to war, which had historically caused so much horror and destruction over the centuries.

As a consequence, the political will to make it work exceeded the economic imperatives that needed to be applied if this was to happen. There was no stated intent for there to be a transfer economy throughout Europe in the same way that the successful currency unions employ in the United Kingdom and the United States of America. Rather, each nation was to retain most of its sovereignty although it was accepted that elements would have be ceded to the centre. Economic management though remained the responsibility of the nation state and to recognise this, the Maastricht Treaty set out three criteria that would apply before a country could join the euro.

These were:

- No excessive budget deficits

- No monetary financing of budget deficits, i.e. unlimited credit to the government from central banks

- No bail outs if a euro-based government were to become insolvent

It was recognised that this was in the main what was missing from the 19th century Latin Currency Union, which collapsed under the weight of national deficits and countries not following the rules. In its enthusiasm to sign up as many members as possible, Europe then proceeded to allow many, if not most, countires to break the rules regardless, so keen was it to bring about the ultimate political union.

The criteria were essential as they would in effect mean that each economy within a nation would be acting the same as the others, thus making more or less a same speed economy for the whole of the eurozone.

Unfortunately for the project, the criteria were simply ignored if the country wished to join. As most countries saw themselves exchanging their weak currencies for the power of the German Deutschmark and French franc, they were only too happy to sign up. The conversion rates were thus set at the wrong level for many countries because once in, had the conversion been possible in reverse, the rate would have been much less as the real economies, which did not meet the criteria, were now tied to a currency which in effect was the German Deutschmark. Interest rates were set in the main for French and particularly German industry and the euro became worth less than the Deutschmark would have been in the same situation, dragged down by the non-performing peripheral countries. As a result, the peripherals became less competitive whilst Germany became more so. The result is yet to be seen, but mathematically, the end of the currency in the form that it is now, cannot be far off. **(10 marks)**

(b) When currencies float, they find their own level according to the market. Thus, they can devalue or revalue in line with the economy of the country involved. If a country's competitiveness is reduced due to business failures, or inflation, the markets will desert the currency and it will decline in value. As a result, its remaining products become relatively cheaper to international customers and people will want to import them. Ultimately it is likely to be a good thing. Once this ability is lost though, the country is tied into an exchange rate that the markets set for the whole of the Union, not just the underperformers, or the high performers. As a result it is almost impossible to restore competitiveness unless the unified currency declines in value significantly. This will not happen though as the effect of strong and weak economies will flatten out any such effect and the true rate that should apply for example to Ireland and Greece, will never be arrived at due to the competitiveness of and demand for German goods, which have to be paid for in euros. Thus to be so tied in, over a period of time, is turning out to be a disaster which is destroying the weaker countries and cannot be resolved, without a unified economy across Europe, which is the next thing to a nation state. This is unlikely to be accepted by many, if any, of the nations involved. **(5 marks)**

PRACTICE EXAMINATION 3

Question 1

Required

In the context of your studies on taxation, consider the statement by Andrew Jackson (7th President of the USA 1767-1845).

'The wisdom of man never yet contrived a system of taxation that would operate with perfect equality.'

(30 marks)

(TOTAL 30 MARKS)

Question 2

Required

(a) Assemble the component parts of the National Debt, commenting briefly on each. **(5 marks)**

(b) Distinguish the differences between raising money for the government by taxation as opposed to the government borrowing the funds by issuing bonds. **(5 marks)**

(c) Explain how inflation reduces the real value of the national debt. **(5 marks)**

(TOTAL 15 MARKS)

Question 3

Required

(a) Discuss the statement 'Northern Rock was a disaster waiting to happen'. **(8 marks)**

(b) Justify the proposition that Bradford and Bingley bank was recklessly managed. **(12 marks)**

(TOTAL 20 MARKS)

Question 4

Required

This question concerns the Report of the Independent Commission on Banking (ICB or the Vickers Report).

(a) Analyse the ring fencing arrangements that it proposes. **(6 marks)**

(b) Justify the recommendations of the Report as they relate to competition and Lloyds Banking Group. **(6 marks)**

(c) Discuss the main criticisms aimed at the Report? **(8 marks)**

(TOTAL 20 MARKS)

Question 5

Required

(a) Critically reflect upon the trend for bank mergers in the 1990s and demonstrate how all the hoped for benefits did not always materialise. **(10 marks)**

(b) Examine why the trend towards Building Society mergers is likely to continue in the future. **(5 marks)**

(TOTAL 15 MARKS)

Answer 1

Taxation is the compulsory taking of money by a government from the governed, either to fund public expenditure or to manipulate the economy. It is usually unpopular because by paying tax, people have to give up either the acquisition of assets or forego some form of consumption. It is inevitable that everyone would rather spend or acquire themselves, rather than give it away to the government, so taxation tends to be unpopular.

The levying of tax always tries to ensure, partly for political reasons (the government wants to get re-elected) and partly for ethical reasons, that it is done in a fair and equitable way. That is to say, people are treated equally and fairly; but this rarely works. The trouble is that however taxation is raised, people would on the whole rather not pay it and most people try to find a way not to do so. What makes it more unpopular is a perception that it is unfair or that individuals perceive that they have been unfairly treated.

Tax can be raised in two ways, directly or indirectly. Direct taxes directed towards individuals, businesses and other entities. A good example of a direct tax is income tax. Indirect taxes are those which still have to be paid, but whose effect is not as noticeable as they are 'hidden'. A good example of an indirect tax is VAT; you only pay it when you buy a commodity. If you wish to avoid it, then you simply do not buy the commodity.

Adam Smith in his *Wealth of Nations (1776)* suggested that tax should be equal on all people paying it, needs to be known about as does the amount, convenient in terms of how it is paid and it should be used for the public benefit. The question asks us to concentrate on the equality of taxation.

Because everyone is different, it is impossible to levy a tax equally on all people, so to that extent, Andrew Jackson's quotation is correct. There is though a general acceptance that a tax ought to be linked to the ability of an individual to pay. This thinking is also extended to the concept that the proportion of income paid as tax should rise as income increases. This is generally applied to income tax and is known as a progressive tax, in that it progresses as income rises.

The opposite, a regressive tax, places a larger proportion of the burden on the less well off. Just because someone earns twice as much as another does not mean that they buy twice as much in terms of taxed commodities, so they do not pay more indirect tax, item for item bought in comparison with their incomes.

Although a progressive tax such as income tax can follow incomes and is liked by politicians for that reason, it is not always equal. This is partly because people can find ways round it (there has been much in the press about people forming companies to employ them rather than being employed directly) and partly because even when rates are supposedly set to catch incomes as they increase, there can be occasions when it simply does not work. The 10p tax rate in the UK is a classic example of this, when it was abolished people on lower incomes ended up paying more.

Politicians also like some regressive taxes as their presence ensures that even poor people who pay no progressive tax, end up paying some tax on goods that they buy. We have already seen that regressive taxes tend to penalise those on lower incomes, the more they buy, so again, there is a lack of equality.

It is easy to try to ensure that tax is equally charged, or at least fairly charged to all people, but in practice whilst the fair intent may be there, there is inevitably inequality and thus at the least perceived, if not actual, unfairness in the outcome. **(30 marks)**

Answer 2

(a) Government stocks otherwise known as gilts, are simply certificates that are issued by the government which can be traded on the stock market at the market rate. They acknowledge that a sum of money has been loaned to the government.

National savings. These are the various types of savings products subscribed to by the public offered by the government via National Savings and Investments (NS & I).

The foreign currency debt. This is made up of bonds and notes issued by the government (just as with the first category) in exchange for loans in foreign currencies. **(5 marks)**

(b) There are two main differences. If a government taxes its people, then that amount of money is taken from them and their wealth is reduced accordingly. If though a government borrows using bonds, provided they are on competitive terms with corporate bonds (i.e. they pay more or less the same coupon) then the wealth of the population is not decreased. However, in return for this advantage, the government has to pay the coupon, which can only come from future taxation, which of course reduces the wealth of the nation, or by borrowing more, which makes the situation worse as it all has to be paid for and ultimately repaid.

If taxation rather than borrowing were to be used to fund the whole of the government's needs, it would reduce consumption and thus make the economy at least grow less or possibly contract. On the other hand, use of borrowing competes for funds with private industry which might find itself short as a result and thus produce less. This can bring about the transfer of the burden of repaying or servicing the national debt onto future generations. The Treasury has to walk a fine line between the two methods of raising money. **(5 marks)**

(c) Inflation only reduces that part of the national debt which is not index linked. Such parts as the NS&I index linked products do not reduce in value. However, this aside, as inflation erodes the value of money, more is in circulation and therefore more tax (particularly indirect and regressive taxes) is received and more borrowing can be made, to account for this qualitative difference. As a result, the value of the national debt declines in line with inflation, although the quantitative size of the debt does not. Of course, as more is borrowed, its size chases inflation, but it is always behind it. Inflation therefore helps a government in the reduction of the national debt. **(5 marks)**

Answer 3

(a) Northern Rock was run by someone who was not a qualified banker who grew the bank too fast, using a business model that relied on borrowed funds from the wholesale market, rather than using the professionally accepted method of placing reliance upon deposits to fund lending and accepting that slower growth but solidity would generate the best results.

It had only 76 branches and they were localised mainly in the North East of England. They simply did not give adequate catchment for deposits to grow the bank to match its chief executive's ambition. It provided 100% + mortgage loans relatively cheaply, in effect, buying market share to grow the size of its assets. It consequently had very limited cash resources to act as a liquidity cushion if the wholesale funds were to dry up. Its problems became evident when the London inter-bank market stopped lending to each other for fear as to where the so-called 'toxic assets' were. Ironically, NR had none of these, not having securitised its assets, but the market simply did not trust anyone at that point. Once this lack of cash became public knowledge, a run occurred, the first on a British bank in 150 years. **(8 marks)**

(b) Bradford & Bingley was a well-respected and long established Building Society which demutualised in 2000 to find itself with 1,000,000 shareholders. Suddenly, it had to answer to the markets for its performance rather than its former mutual members who were happy with their steady income from interest. The markets were less likely to be so docile, but no-one appears to have seen this essential difference. The management remained the same now that it was a bank, but it was doing rather different things.

It had to perform better in financial terms and its management became, as happened with Northern Rock and RBS, obsessed with size for its own sake. Consequently it went into the buy-to-let market, encouraging existing house owners to use their equity as security for additional properties which they could then rent out. The theory put forward was that each would pay for the next, although in reality it was very similar to a pyramid selling scheme; there simply were not enough people wanting to rent for it to be sustainable in the long term.

It also bought mortgages from other lenders to grow its book and make its assets larger in terms of quantity, but little effort was made in terms of quality of assets. Worse, still trying to grow its numbers, it lent for house purchases at over 100% and allowed self-certification, with the inevitable result that its customers simply lied as to what they earned, sometimes inflating their income considerably. Few questions were asked and the result was that the mortgage book grew, but with some very dodgy assets.

The buy-to-let market declined considerably with the arrival of the banking crisis and prices of the properties against which money was lent declined. The whole of the buy-to-let business was based upon the astonishing presumption that house prices always went up. The truism that they sometimes go down was simply ignored. Thus, the bank found itself with a considerable amount of unsecured debt and customers who simply could not repay what they had borrowed. Even if the security was realised, a considerable loss would be incurred by the bank.

As a result, if found it very difficult to raise money on the London market, particularly given the general condition of inter-bank lending, let alone the results of its own reckless lending. It tried to raise capital with a new issue in the Summer of 2008 which failed and this in turn destroyed what little confidence remained in the bank by the public and the markets. Its share price collapsed and it simply ran out of cash.

All of this was a direct result of demutualisation, an obsession with size at any cost and being run by people who simply did not know what they were doing (who were not qualified!). Reckless does not do it justice. **(12 marks)**

Answer 4

(a) The ring fencing proposals are designed to segregate the retail and investment operations of the banks. Under these the retail operations will be a separate body corporate from the rest of the bank with its own board. Any dividends made will be paid to the parent organisation, which will own all the shares in the retail subsidiary. Thus, it will be protected to a large degree from the global markets by this separate incorporation although it will be able to lend as before to large corporate customers and use derivatives to hedge its own positions. It will be required to retain a 10% core capital ratio as a prudential matter, rather than the 7% envisaged by Basle III.

This is intended to protect the depositors funds, so that they are only used for pure banking purposes, rather than them being mixed up with funds from the investment banking side of the bank and being used to undertake so called 'casino banking'. There is no objection to the bank risking its own funds for this purpose, but not those of its customers. If the investment arm were to go under as a result of bad investments, the separate corporate nature of the retail operation would protect it from doing the same, which is what would happen if they all traded under one corporate umbrella. **(6 marks)**

(b) The Report decided that LBG did not need to sell more than the 632 of its branches that it had agreed to as a condition of state support. The intention was that these would be bought by the Co-operative Bank, which would place it in a similar position competition wise to the other major banking groups, RBS, LBG, HSBC and Barclays. However, the Co-op bank group was plunged into crisis in November 2013 when they revealed they would need an extra £1.5 billion to recapitalise the bank.

The Report also recommended that a new system needed to be created to permit both personal and business customers to move their current accounts to a competitor within seven days due to the considerable difficulties that thousands of customers currently experience when transferring accounts. These difficulties, which may be intentional or due to lethargy or lack of interest as the account is moving in any case, are seen to inhibit customers from changing banks and a system that works, common to all banks, is needed to enable customers to move if they wish with as little trouble as possible. The ICB felt that this would encourage competition as so few people currently change, it is thought because of the difficulties involved. **(6 marks)**

(c) The main criticisms came from the banks in the main who did not like the ring fencing proposals. This may have been because they wished to continue gambling with customers' money, or because of the costs that the proposal will incur or both. They did though point out that the ring fencing would not have stopped Northern Rock's problems which were entirely down to appalling management or the crazy merger between RBS and ABN-Amro. They felt that even if there was a ring fence as proposed, the public would not recognised this and still 'run' on the retail arm if the investment arm failed. To some degree this has been proved by the ring fenced UK Santander, which has experienced higher than average withdrawals in the wake of the rumours about its corporately separate Spanish parent.

The costs of ring fencing are estimated at between £4 and £8bn which will inevitably have to be obtained somehow from customers. There was also a suggestion that it would inhibit productivity and reduce the GDP by one or two billion pounds.

Some people have also suggested that the Report went for easy options rather than requiring the break-up of the big banks generally.

The jury remains out on the validity or otherwise of these ideas, regrettably its decision can only be proved either way were another bank to fail. **(8 marks)**

Answer 5

(a) In the latter part of the 1980s British banks became amongst the most successful in the world. Five of the world's fifteen largest banks were British. None the less, they were under intense pressure to deliver increasingly better results and the more successful they were, the more this pressure grew.

Although reduced costs did not deliver revenue, they did have the potential to increase profits, albeit perhaps on a once only basis as costs could only be reduced so much. Staff were disposed of to a point where some might say things became dangerous as expertise ebbed away and this has had to be replaced by IT. In many cases this turned out to be as expensive as the staff which it had hoped to replace.

The other big source of costs was the branch network, which IT did have a big chance of not perhaps replacing, but certainly permitting many to be closed and the network consolidated to a core. At the same time, mergers would mean that duplicate branches could close and the same or more business be done, at a much reduced cost. Therefore the 1990s saw a trend towards branch closures and mergers of banks.

A clash of management styles in the newly merged banks, bad leadership, obsession with growth at any cost, poor or contradictory planning, constant change and so on all led to the expected massive savings (one US study suggested as much as 20%) simply not happening. The banks apparent mania with change and knee jerk responses to deliver quick wins resulted often in some of the changes being undone, parts of the banks being sold off sometimes several times across many buyers and sellers. Staff morale dropped as constant change and change of purpose resulted in lack of direction and confidence.

The larger asset bases which resulted from mergers meant that shareholders looked for better returns, which in many cases were not forthcoming and by 2008, the latest management incumbents started to recognise that mergers for what sometimes seemed their own sake on the basis that they always delivered savings (wouldn't they?) were no longer the norm. For such to happen, they had to be justified in terms of adding value to the shareholders which meant increased dividends and share prices. It was unfortunate that it had taken some serious problems such as those which RBS and its huge number of takeovers and the Lloyds TSB Halifax Bank of Scotland mergers to show such up for the folly that they often were. **(10 marks)**

(b) Many building societies de-mutualised and turned into banks. It says something for their management that none remain as independent organisations. None the less, the remaining mutuals have continued to reduce in number as larger concerns have taken over the smaller ones. Sometimes this has been for simple operational reasons, such as the Dunfermline which got involved in a hugely expensive and in the end unmanageable IT project, but others have merged for purely economic reasons.

Increased competition both from other building societies and from other financial institutions may cause smaller, weaker organisations to merge with larger ones, or for smaller ones to merge to create larger organisations. Yorkshire taking over Barnsley, Norwich & Peterborough and Chelsea are all examples of the former.

Smaller societies because of their size may not be able to offer the larger range of products permitted by the Building Societies Act 1986, when in effect, they became small and/or mutual banks. This could encourage them to merge with others, or for takeovers to happen. Similarly they may be put under pressure in terms of capital adequacy, particularly if they grow quickly. No-one wants to be the next Northern Rock. Economies of scale are bound to come in if a takeover/merger happens and they will also help with an administrative burden which can be almost overwhelming to some small societies. Finally, if any small outfits incur losses of any size, this could imperil their cash positions.

For all these reasons, mergers and takeovers are likely to continue, but with care, no-one today wants the recklessness of the 1990s to be repeated and mergers to happen for their own sake. **(5 marks)**